School of Visual Arts
Masters in Branding

Brands in the Age of AI

Mark Kingsley
Series Foreword by Debbie Millman

ROCKPORT

Quarto.com

© 2025 Quarto Publishing Group USA Inc.
Text © 2025 Mark Kingsley

First published in 2025 by Rockport Publishers, an imprint of The Quarto Group,
100 Cummings Center, Suite 265-D, Beverly, MA 01915, USA.
T (978) 282-9590 F (978) 283-2742

EEA Representation, WTS Tax d.o.o.,
Žanova ulica 3, 4000 Kranj, Slovenia.
www.wts-tax.si

Rockport Publishers titles are also available at discount for retail, wholesale,
promotional, and bulk purchase. For details, contact the Special Sales Manager by
email at specialsales@quarto.com or by mail at The Quarto Group, Attn: Special
Sales Manager, 100 Cummings Center, Suite 265-D, Beverly, MA 01915, USA.

10 9 8 7 6 5 4 3 2 1

ISBN: 978-0-7603-9521-9

Digital edition published in 2025
eISBN: 978-0-7603-9522-6

Library of Congress Cataloging-in-Publication Data available

Design: Mark Kingsley
Page Layout: Megan Jones Design
Photography: All images by Mark Kingsley; except where noted. 57, top: US
Department of Defense/National Museum of the U.S. Navy/National Archives;
57, bottom: US Department of Defense/Armed Services Technical Information
Agency; 117: Illustration: Leo Natsume; 121: US General Services Administration;
155: Photography: Seth Mroczka

Printed in Malaysia

For you: the subject in this object.

This series of books is an offering from the School of Visual Arts Masters in Branding Program, the first and longest-running program of its kind in the world. This pioneering course of study provides a select group of graduate students an opportunity to study with some of the most accomplished brand experts working today.

Our intensive one-year graduate degree program is a challenging multi-disciplinary experience of lectures, real-world client projects, and unique and progressive workshops and includes the examination of classic business school case studies, individual one-on-one professional mentorship, and group and personal projects.

The foundation of the Master of Professional Studies in Branding is the deep exploration and understanding of the role brand strategy plays in business, behavior, marketing, and culture. The curriculum allows students to create frameworks to guide brand, design, and business development; critically evaluate brand, business, marketing, and design approaches; and master the intellectual link between strategy and creativity. In addition, we analyze marketing challenges involved in creating, sustaining, and reinventing brands that have fallen out of pace with culture. In a sentence, we work hard.

This remarkable series of books gathers together and documents the brand research and pedagogy we've been investigating and creating over the past fifteen years. The very faculty that have invented and developed this curriculum have codified their learning and their teaching for the first time in this manner.

We are proud to share this work with the world and with you.

Debbie Millman
Chair, Masters in Branding
School of Visual Arts

Contents

Introduction

How does one resist a magic incantation? Ulysses ordered his men to fill their ears with wax to resist the spell of the Sirens' song. He also had himself bound to the mast of their ship so he could hear the song. The sailors kept to their tasks without interruption, while Ulysses was tortured with desire.

Today's siren call is Artificial Intelligence (AI). And the possibility for semi-magical incantations (otherwise known as prompts) to bring forth never-before-seen wonders is equally seductive to all players in contemporary society. What follows is an exploration of the effects of AI on the consumers, creators, and observers of brands and brand phenomena. It is neither an act of resistance, nor a tribute. It is also not a precise technical document. It is about brands, which are ultimately about feelings and associations, whether they are perfectly accurate or not. Hopefully it will be seen as respectful observation and helpful guidance.

But first, we need a method.

As humanity further enters the digital realm, our experiences become more symbolic. While our feelings and responses will always be embodied and immediate—the heart flutter of love, exhaustion after a long day, hunger and thirst—the increasing cognitive demands of

Opposite: The siren call of AI.

modern life—political alignment, shopping selections, opinions about music—require some shorthanded way to make those choices easier. This is the utility of brands.

Brands act as quick, easy handles with which to grasp complex ideas. Instead of making time to spend with a companion, free of responsibilities and distractions, with the possibility of either sex or finishing off a pint of ice cream, we "Netflix and chill." And instead of saying that an image was enhanced and altered, we say it was photoshopped—to the chagrin of Adobe's legal team.

So in a very basic sense, brands are a series of cognitive steps toward a desired outcome: meaning. And therein lies the synergistic relationship between brands and the digital realm, which is composed of algorithms. Similar to a brand, an algorithm is a series of commands used to solve a specific problem or produce a desired outcome.

The ability of algorithms to take in data, then "learn" from that basis to complete tasks and processes, has brought the once-theorized ideal of AI closer to reality. We are still quite a ways off from an Artificial Generalized Intelligence (AGI) which matches, or, in the case of superintelligence (ASI), bests human abilities. But on the lower cognitive level, the current applications of AI in predictive analytics and machine learning have displayed astonishing capabilities within a short period of time. They are entering the "uncanny valley," i.e., the point where algorithmic output evokes a human emotional response.

Still, we need to remember that algorithms are calculations; and that the tasks they are asked to perform are calculative in nature. We do A in order to accomplish B, which then allows us to reach C. Successful returns on investment, profit and loss gains, upward quarterly projections, accurate Gantt charts, and tight delivery schedules are easily rewarded because they are objectively trackable and verified. This mechanistic process is an expression of *calculative thinking*, the product of a worldview of cause, effect, data, and tactics. And calculative thinking is perhaps the greatest belief system of modern humanity, with its pleasures of progress, measured growth, and accomplishment.

Calculative thinking is also concerned with efficiency, which is the focus of the current state of AI development. New York University marketing professor and public speaker Scott Galloway calls AI "corporate Ozempic"—another brand-as-cognitive-handle—to describe

Opposite: An algorithm is a series series of commands or steps executed in order to arrive at a desired outcome.

the quick weight loss-like ability of companies to reduce their workforce with AI. What used to take days, months, or even years of work, now is achieved in a fraction of the time. Predictive algorithmic patterning of protein folds is already changing the speed and accuracy of drug development, bioengineering, and alternative fuel development. And machine learning can target personalized marketing messages at scale. In an increasing number of areas, the decision-making process is better outsourced to an algorithm. And generally, a brand's audience and producer sees subsequent benefits.

But there is still room for improvement. AI output can sometimes seem like the result of a kind of aphasia. Soon after launching, Google's *AI Overviews* feature suggested adding non-toxic glue for cheese to stick to pizza dough. Where experts in philology (the study of the history of language) or the diagnosis of brain diseases might make the connection between "glue" and "gluten," the average person suffers the gap between theory and lived experience, and how much more work is needed before the product is efficient, accurate, *and* reliable.

As developers and users rush to get ahead of AI's growing presence, all eyes are on the calculative details. What are the best prompting practices? How can a creative person's style be monetized once it is used to train a generative platform? How do we untangle copyright when AI-generated material is used for profit? How can data rise above connective observations into true insights? All valuable questions, but limited to calculative thinking.

If we are to make sense of our place in the digital realm, we need to consider the implications of such a move across all aspects of human existence. AI's arrival will have corresponding step changes affecting our relationships with time, space, history, knowledge, institutions, cultural narratives, and the world. In other words, AI is a metaphysical shift. And a way to access these new relationships is through contemplative thinking.[1] Such thinking is based on traditions outside market-based or computational theories, ones which might include sociology, critical theory, anthropology, philosophy, ethics, poetry, and so on.

Regardless of the deepening cybernetic connections to our devices, we remain human, not mere things. And though our interactions will become increasingly mediated by AI systems and avatars, we will continue to interact with others in our contradictory, random, paradoxical,

Opposite: Google's *AI Overviews* suggested using nontoxic glue for cheese to stick to pizza dough.

magical humanity. That very messiness elevates us above mindless consumption, and is the source for all the joys and surprises of life. So what follows must be more contemplative than calculative, focusing on how brands might make human life more fulfilling, more connected, more attuned to our impact on the planet, and less transactional.

Goals for This Book

First off, this is a book about brands.

There is much commentary on AI. Perhaps too much. And the majority of that commentary favors the calculative. For this, there is infinite demand. As soon as one types a word of analysis in this environment, the idea is obsolete five minutes later, and the need for updated analysis returns.

If one is to go through the effort to write or read a book on the relationship between AI and brands, perhaps the more sustainable path is one that explores what that relationship reveals about the other. We all have preconceptions about both AI and the concept of branding, and there is a potential for each to be transformed in that exploration. Engaging in this dialogue in book form offers the space to shore up our definitions and clarify where certain ideas come from. In the case of this book, and after a lifetime of reading and experience—not all on AI—the theme of *subjectivity* seems to be a valuable territory. While that may initially seem trivial, if one dives into the structures of consciousness, the attempts to create an artificial intelligence, and how that is deployed in a brand sense, **subjectivity** becomes a useful framework. One that is more personal, and has more potential impact on individuals than the current favorite topic of authenticity.

Therefore, while the case studies and examples that follow are destined to become artifacts of the past, they describe a contingency where brands attend to that aspect of subjectivity through the application of AI. The future is the result of collective actions. And if we consider the potential effect of our contemplative and active lives, the hope remains for a world built with a sense of mutual care.

1   See: *Mark Kingsley, "Thinking Design Thinking," in *The Education of a Design Writer*, edited by Steven Heller & Molly Heintz (Allworth, 2025).

Opposite: Subjectivity is the quality of being seen as a person, rather than as another object in the world.

Injunction

In 1985, Dr. Edward de Bono, who coined the term "lateral thinking," published *Six Thinking Hats*. In it, the metaphor of colored hats was used to identify the different functions of team members. The White Hat role is concerned with "just the facts, ma'am"; the optimistic Yellow Hat searches for positive benefit; the Red Hat explores feelings and intuition; the Green Hat focuses on creativity; and the Blue Hat facilitates or manages. The most powerful Hat, the Black Hat, lives in the pessimistic realm of risks, dangers, and cynicism. It is the most powerful Hat because of its ability to derail. And when confronted with something new, it is the Hat people immediately reach for.

There is, and will be, much commentary on AI's destructive wake as it decimates workforces, demands increasing amounts of power to run its servers, homogenizes culture to the center, and surveils people to either maximize profit or maintain power (commonly known as "surveillance capitalism"). Such results come from calculative thinkers focused on extraction: the extraction of resources, the extraction of mindshare, the extraction of efficiencies, and the extraction of lives lived richly—all for the sake of wealth and control. Shun them, for they exploit the lesser demons of our nature and work to separate people from each other.

This book is an effort to explore possibilities, with an eye toward the potential for brands to enhance the collective flourishing of human existence, as reframed and enabled through AI. It is not a condemnation of profit or healthy returns, but rather a plea to keep the needs of others in mind. Make people happy, the money will come. So for now, let's try to not wear that Black Hat.

Definitions and Limitations: Toward Subjectivity

Before we proceed with our meditative thought, It might be helpful to clarify a few terms and establish basic territories. While those working in AI development speak with each other in a specific technical jargon, the rising tide of "expert" practitioners working in the fields of design, advertising, branding, and strategy use a mixed vocabulary of the local vernacular and trade language. So as we search for the right metaphors to describe AI and its effects, a common lexicon seems necessary. And by defining terms that are often used almost unconsciously, perhaps we might build a strong foundation for us to understand the role of AI in our branded society and how it connects to brand phenomena.

The goal of this exercise is to find an opening into how AI might be used to enhance brand relationships, and not as a way to extract more profit or attention. The grand proposal for this book is to surpass the current gold standard of authenticity—one built on trust, familiarity, and resonance—into a greater level of subjectivity. In other words, when an authentic brand relationship allows one to engage, we give ourselves permission to join or purchase. Any emotional work or outcome is contained within the consumer. And to the brand, the consumer remains objectified. But in a subjective relationship, the consumer feels like they are, to use current parlance, "seen." There is a comfort in the shared recognition of one's own experience, and as an individual mind with independent agency. This is where the potential lies for AI in branding: in the combination of computational power, database integration, predictive algorithms, and (most importantly) good faith.

One must insist on good faith.

There are many ways to describe technology. At its most basic level, it is an expression of human action that is not limited to machinery or instrumentation. Technology is what we do, and how we dwell upon the earth. So for our purposes, let's define technology as "the extension of our being."

In other words, a hammer extends one's arm, a telescope extends one's vision, the wheel extends one's range, and so on. Stanley Kubrick's 1968 film *2001: A Space Odyssey* makes a rather good argument that the origin of technology was an animal bone used as a club. And if one looks to the archeological record, the earliest known use of stone tools by pre-homo sapiens hominins dates to more than three million years ago. Using the objects around us is how we dwell on Earth.

But what if technology's origins cannot be found in the archeological record? What if our first technology was language itself? In that case, language extends our lived experience. It allows one to report observed resources (food, water, animal herds), to warn of danger, or organize a hunting party around particular animal behavior. And once we have the basics of indexing the world, new linguistic opportunities reveal themselves—communal hierarchies, task assignments, and religion— which in turn allow us to reframe how we understand our immediate surroundings, social groups, our thoughts, and nature itself. So then, technology is no longer a "thing." Instead, it is the act of reframing the objects at hand, whether it be an animal bone, a combustion engine, or a forest. Once we figure out that a waterwheel dipped in a river can turn a millstone, it's only a few conceptual steps more before the same river is driving the turbines of a hydroelectric dam. What was once a feature of a landscape is now seen as a source of power.

In that light, technology is not the opposite of nature, but its reframing. And to push this idea a bit further, if one of the structural qualities of language comes from its ability to capture difference (here/there, up/ down, in/out, etc.) then perhaps nature itself didn't exist in our minds until we identified that which was not man-made as nature.

This dovetails nicely into an idea from Aristotle that the material found in nature is at rest, and it is only human artifice (from the Latin roots for "art" and "make") that transforms (reframes) it into articles and artifacts. And because, according to Aristotle, nature is incomplete, human artifice, in a sense, "completes" nature.

Opposite: The origins of technology may have involved animal bones and stone tools.

It may seem strange to blur the lines between nature and technology in this manner, but we do not exist in a state where mind and matter are separate. That dualism is a vestige of Cartesian thinking, which, to be honest, contributed greatly to human development but doesn't fully capture the interconnectedness of our existence.

Cartesian Thinking and Dualism

One November night in 1619, René Descartes sat by the fire in his winter dressing gown, looked down at his hands and wondered if they were real. Or were they and his body the deception of a "malicious, powerful, cunning demon?" After a bit of meditation, he came to the realization that there is "never any reliable way of distinguishing being awake from being asleep." All that he perceived was to be doubted, including his perceptions.

But Descartes saw that his doubt was a form of thinking. He was a thinking thing, and his essence consisted solely in being a thinking thing. His thinking did not extend to being in a body. Therefore he was certain that he was distinct from his body and could exist without it.[1]

While not the first, Descartes' *Meditations* is commonly seen as *the* origin point of mind/body dualism in Western thinking, where the mind and body, or better yet, mind and matter, are distinct and separate. And while the mind has no physical substance, matter does. And it is constantly in motion.

Dualism appears constantly in human society, whether it be social constructs of gender, the binary code of ones and zeros flowing through computer systems, the true and false states of Boolean logic, or the way in which *we-as-subjects* view everything and everyone else as objects. We built our world via dualism.

Legend has it that Descartes preferred to stay in bed late. And one morning, he looked up and saw a fly crawling on the ceiling, which caused him to wonder how one might accurately locate it in space. He determined that if one of the corners was established as a reference point, he then had an X/Y axis which could establish a gridded coordinate system in two dimensions. And if you add a Z axis, the result is a coordinate system that can locate objects in three-dimensional space.

Opposite: The origin of mind/body dualism in Western thinking began when René Descartes sat by the fire and looked down at his hands. (Likeness modeled after Frans Hals' *Portret van René Descartes*, 1649)

The Cartesian coordinate system connected geometry to algebra, which is the use of mathematical statements to describe relationships between things that vary. Such variables include things like supply and price relationships, financial projections, determining correct medicine dosage in relation to an individual's biological factors, or the trajectories of matter through space. In Descartes' worldview, objects existed in and of themselves, and in relation to each other. Everything could be described mathematically, through what came to be known as analytical geometry.

But the Cartesian coordinate system is only one iteration in humanity's long history of projecting structure onto a chaotic universe. A simpler version would be the grid. And contrary to adherents of Swiss modernism in graphic design, or mid-twentieth-century architecture, our most "modernist" of systems is as old as human society. Early examples can be traced back to around 2600 BCE, where archeological sites in contemporary Pakistan reveal gridded urban planning. And if one thinks of it, the massive stone blocks of the Egyptian Pyramids are a form of grid as well.

Cartesian/gridded thinking allowed us to maximize, discover, and (often) overexploit both natural and human resources. In 1784, the United States government approved Thomas Jefferson's plan to overlay a rectilinear grid across what was then the western section of the new nation. Today's American landscape looks totally different from the air than when flying over any other country. The insistence of a relentless, abstract mathematical order persists, regardless of mountain ranges, bodies of water, differences in soil, or the presence of indigenous populations (they too were absorbed by the grid). The landscape is a continual patchwork of rectangles and grids. Circles do appear, but they are the result of centralized irrigation methods and still conform to the grid. In this case, the battle of mind over matter tilts toward the mind.

And because technology is a kind of reframing, consider how we apply grid technology to the most nebulous resource: time. Any employee

Above: One way that people situate themselves in a chaotic universe is via the Cartesian coordinate system.

Opposite: Both consciousness and a street corner can be described as the experience of a confluence of forces.

whose work is based on shifts or productivity targets, and anyone mapping out tasks over time with a Gantt chart have all succumbed to the cartesian demand.

Consciousness

There is a nice, sharp clarity to seeing the world logically, where the various qualities of phenomena are crisply accounted for and can be both described and predicted. But everyday existence differs.

We maintain a subject/object relationship to the things which we have elevated to the category of worth-being-cared-about: house keys, smartphones, shoes, coffee. Yet when we walk across our bedroom floor to fetch our house keys and smartphone, are we really concerned with the floor's solidity? No. We take it for granted and just walk.

Consciousness is much more than the navigation of dualistic subject/ object operations. It is virtual—you can't touch it—but it is realized and has influence in the world, such as software or money. And it doesn't automatically guarantee intelligence or agency. As the German cognitive scientist and philosopher Joscha Bach jokes: "You don't get conscious after the Ph.D., you become conscious before you can track a finger."[2]

Bach, his professor Dietrich Dörner, and language philosopher Philip Johnson-Laird make compelling cases for looking at consciousness as a computational model, not as an action of a computer, per se, but within some sort of computational, or better yet, conditional framework. But models are always suspect because they tend to be reductive. And anyone proposing a model of consciousness is suspect because they are working inside the system of consciousness itself.

So in the spirit of suspect proposals, perhaps we could think of consciousness not as one thing, but *our lived experience* of a confluence of several (many) forces yet-to-be-determined. They could be conditional, energetic, gravitational, a form of quantum entanglement, extra-dimensional, or the mysteries of dark matter. Whatever they are, they combine into the experience we call consciousness, whose very simplicity is what makes it so complex. Just like a street corner.

A street corner is also the gathering of many forces: vehicles passing through, turning, stopping for others, a meeting point, a business address, a dividing point between neighborhoods or voting districts, an ideal location for a busker, the place where certain laws and regulations are in play, or a personal metaphor on a bad day where a beautiful sunset seen after turning a corner acts as a reminder to live, laugh, and love.

The theorist (and ex-music publicist) Howard Bloom has an elegant metaphor he calls a "recruitment strategy." When we look at a wave, we know that the water molecules aren't all traveling hundreds of miles to that point. They're mostly moving up and down as the energy of "waveness" passes through that location. That energy is a recruitment strategy, known as a wave.

Extending that metaphor, companies are not static collections of individuals. People join and leave constantly, but the company doesn't change its name or core business with each hire or exit. And jazz compositions, whether they're written out beforehand or spontaneously emerge in performance, are recruitment strategies. The performers could be members of an established group, or pickup players in a late-night jam session, both of which are different, but simultaneous, recruitment strategies. As is a company ... as is our street corner ... as is our consciousness.

Opposite: Because it is experienced, consciousness needs to be embodied in some form of a physical manifestation.

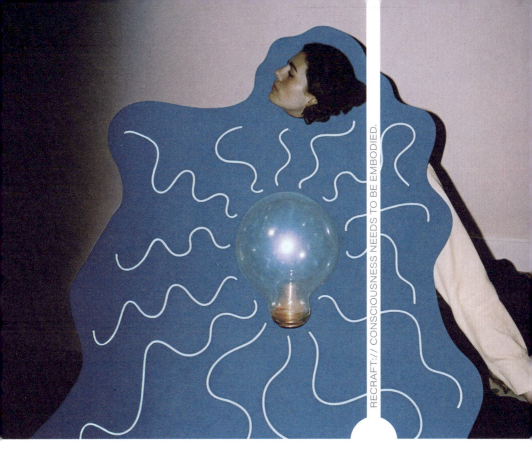

Therefore, consciousness is a recruitment strategy, an "energy," a con-fluence of vectors, but it needs a physical location for it to emerge, like a wave needs water, like our selves need our bodies, and perhaps, like artificial general intelligence needs a server.

We know our consciousness because we experience it. And our percep-tion of both consciousness and the world in general relies on our ability to recognize differences: am I hungry or not? Is this thing in my hands too heavy or can I get it to the car by myself? Do I need to clean my room, or can I let it go a few more days? These indices of difference are both the fundamental building blocks of meaning, and proof of our consciousness.

But here's the interesting thing: consciousness is embodied. It needs a medium, a body, a physical manifestation. But its manifestation does not necessarily need to be centered, like the sense our consciousness is centered in our bodies. While an artificial consciousness could be distributed across a network of servers, it would still need to interact in the real or the virtual.

This way of thinking about consciousness only underscores how far we still have to go to fully understand or describe it. We still don't know what we don't know about gravity, quantum entanglement, string theory, or all the other possibilities that contribute to consciousness. But it does begin to describe what more needs to happen before AGI emerges, or before we can identify it as a form of consciousness.

Intelligence

The ability to acquire a body of information—either through experience, reading, viewing, or listening—and then act positively in the world—with ability, intention, and a measure of responsiveness—is probably the simplest way to define intelligence. Note that this does not limit intelligence to rationality or reason. If consciousness is our experience of the world, it would be a mistaken assumption to limit that feature of reality to rational thought. We encounter reality through the ways in which it matters to us, and not always through reason. This is why we recognize emotional, social, and other forms of intelligence in others, and if we are humble enough, in other living beings and possibly in the emerging forms of artificial intelligence. A dog quickly learns what the sound of a food container being opened means, and just as quickly an algorithm learns whether a user tends to view football highlights or cat videos.

Subjectivity

When we recognize the presence of some form of intelligence, we are acknowledging the subjectivity of an other. In other words, subjectivity is dependent on a mind. And because intelligence is the ability to act upon acquired knowledge, the condition of subjectivity applies to, and describes, an observer. Things which can be confirmed independently of a mind are then described as objective.

Two people can occupy a space where one thinks the room is too cold, and the other says it is too warm. Both are making subjectively true statements. And when they look at the thermostat to read the temperature, the number of degrees on the display is objectively true.

This correlates subjectivity to other forms of intelligence. In the case of our couple occupying a space, if they are in a caring relationship, each will find a way to accommodate the comfort of the other, whether it be by wearing extra layers, dressing in lighter fabrics, or some other arrangement. There is a shared recognition of each person's experience, as individual minds with independent needs and agency.

Opposite: Temperature is experienced subjectively, but measured objectively.

Now that we have a basic understanding of subjectivity, we have a tool to explore where AI overlaps with brand. And if the extension of human presence through technology reframes and reorders the objects in the world, then the technology of AI reframes and reorders how we see brands and branding. **For our usage, the new benchmark for anyone working in brands moves beyond the verification of authenticity into the extension of subjectivity.**

Consciousness is an outward experience. We are always conscious "of." And authenticity is our outward valuation directed at an object. But subjectivity, as we are calling it, is felt on both a conscious and unconscious level. It can be authentic or performative, as long as the recipient feels like their condition or presence has been acknowledged. This is how brands can enter a space where the interaction of databases, machine learning, and design combine to at least give someone a sense of a personalized interaction, unique only to them. The experience moves from an acknowledgement of authenticity—the product is real, the product meets expectations, the product has value—to the moment where the product is "just right, just what I need to make my life, as I define it, better."

The philosopher Martin Buber articulated this simply as the shift from an I-it relationship to an I-Thou. I-it sees each other in the language of demographics and segmentation: annual income, postal code, credit scores, and purchase histories. Once we recognize that we encounter reality not through reason, but through the ways it matters to us, we take the first step to I-Thou. In meeting each other as we are, the value is found in how we live within a mutuality of care. Profit is not fully disregarded, but enhanced and sustained through improved reputation, trust, and loyalty.

Granted, this sense of subjectivity seems more appropriate for a lifestyle brand or a service, but there is room for its application in even the most basic consumer packaged goods (CPG) brands.

1   René Descartes, *Meditations on First Philosophy, in which are demonstrated the existence of God and the distinction between the human soul and the body* (1639).

2   Joscha Bach, "The Case for Conscious AI," presentation to the Institute of Art and Ideas (September 29, 2024).

Opposite: When a product is seen as something that is "just right, just what I need," it then becomes something that matters.

A Perceptual History of AI

A standard procedure when beginning a branding project is to look to the origin story for understanding and inspiration. Knowing where a brand comes from can explain how it's seen today, and confirm any connections (or disconnections) to its "authenticity."

Remember, we can have a brand association with even the most abstract thing. And in our case, AI is such an abstract thing. If governments around the world can write legislation in response to *the possibility* of potential drawbacks, then AI has brand attributes.

For our purposes, the story of AI is a tale of relationships developed over time. And compared to many other brands, AI is associated with a loosely-defined future, even though it is a product of the past. We live in three time frames: the past, the present, and—not the future—but the conditional. Boardrooms love to speak about the future: the promise of the future, future returns, and idealized outcomes. But in reality, the future is a superimposition of possible outcomes in an open field, all of which require certain conditions to be met first. And those conditions reflect people's expectations and ambitions as well as their past behavior.

So in that light, let's consider three simultaneous perceptions of AI: as an agent of efficiency, as a new creative paradigm, and as a soulless apparition. While there are many more perceptions—drilling down into specificities of professions, applications, and outcomes—these three are a good start due to their broad relevance. Technical breakthroughs in logic or execution will be, by necessity, described in equally-as-broad strokes and focus more on their affect than their instrumentality.

Agents of Efficiency

The recent history of AI continues a much longer desire to control or optimize labor and social relations, often in the name of efficiency. To consumers, devices and procedures, ranging from desktop publishing to the ChatGPT platform, save money and open up leisure time. They make life easier. To businesses, process innovations increase productivity, reduce costs, and lessen labor requirements. They make activity more profitable. Whether such efficiencies are beneficial or detrimental depends on which side of the equation one stands.

In this light, three figures stand out because process innovation and basic computation benefitted from their work: the French weaver and merchant Joseph Marie Jacquard (1752–1834), English mathematician and inventor Charles Babbage (1791–1871), and mathematician and writer Ada Lovelace (1815–1852).

Jacquard was one of the first to apply a binary on/off approach to manufacturing. To achieve specific patterns and designs on industrial textile looms, certain courses of threads are raised over another course and a shuttle transports a cross-thread across the loom. Then another set is raised for the next step in the pattern, and the shuttle heads back to where it started. Very quickly, weaving a bolt of cloth while keeping track of where you are in the pattern becomes a mental challenge.

Before Jacquard, Basile Bouchon and his assistant Jean-Baptiste Falcon's system used a paper roll with punched holes to trigger specific courses of thread—just like a player piano. While it relieved the tedium of manual and mental operation, it still required two operators: one for the loom and one for the paper roll.

Twenty years later, Jacques de Vaucanson, known at the time as an inventor of automatons, was charged with reforming the silk manufacturing process in France. At the time, textile manufacturing was one of the main drivers of the Industrial Revolution, and a significant contributor to the French economy. In 1792, France imported 29 million livres (a unit of measurement loosely equivalent to a pound) of raw silk. So any way to improve production was of national importance.

Vaucanson replaced Bouchon's paper rolls with a series of punch cards, an innovation that Jacquard perfected fifty years later by increasing the number of threads controlled at each step, which resulted in a

Opposite: Joseph Marie Jacquard's punch cards increased the "computational" ability of 19th Century French looms and were an important innovation in the history of computing hardware.

more elaborate finished product. Simply put, Jacquard increased the "computational" ability of the system. And the interchangeability of card series allowed operators to "reprogram" looms much faster than the previous turnaround time of days.

While the history of calculating machines can be traced back to the second century BCE, the work of English mathematician and inventor Charles Babbage represented a conceptual breakthrough. At the time, "human computers" calculated numerical tables which were used in science, engineering, and navigation. Because they were calculated, and transcribed by hand, they were subject to inaccuracies.

In 1822, Babbage published a proposal for a device he called the Difference Engine. Named from the "divided differences" algorithm used in its function, the Difference Engine was designed to tabulate polynomial functions, equations with variables familiar to anyone who has studied algebra. Polynomial functions are used in domains ranging from algebra, chemistry, physics, economics, numerical analysis, and social science. Compared to today's computers, Babbage's Difference Engine was much simpler and slower—a basic calculator. But it did promise faster and accurate calculations than were currently achievable. The British government was interested and helped fund its development.

As he was building his prototype, Babbage visited a number of factories and workshops. This experience was captured in *On the Economy of Machinery and Manufactures*, published in 1832. The book analyzed manufacturing processes within an economic context, and produced what is known as the "Babbage Principle." It points out how dividing labor into specialized tasks which are based on skill level can significantly reduce production costs by utilizing each worker's output more efficiently. There are similar motifs (the economies of employee training, for example) in Frederick Winslow Taylor's *Principles of Scientific Management*, and Karl Marx relied on Babbage when developing his theories on technology and industry.

After the death of his wife and father in the same year, Babbage inherited a considerable amount of money and began to host Saturday night soirées, where a small model of the Difference Engine was on display. One evening in 1832, the 18-year-old daughter of poet Lord Byron, Ada Lovelace, attended a soirée with her mother and charmed Babbage enough for him to invite them the next day for a demonstration. This sparked in her an interest in mathematics and Babbage's work.

Opposite: A model of Charles Babbage's Difference Engine.

Eight years later, Babbage traveled to Turin, Italy, and presented a lecture series on the Engine's principles. One of the attendees, Luigi Menabrea, wrote and published an account of the events in French. The English physicist and inventor Sir Charles Wheatstone suggested to Lovelace that she translate the report, which she did. Looking for a way to contribute to the Difference Engine project, and encouraged by Babbage's suggestion that she add an appendix, she wrote an additional 42 pages on top of the initial 25 page translation. The last appendix, known as "Note G," was a "diagram for the computation by the Engine of the Numbers of Bernoulli." Bernoulli numbers are a sequence of rational numbers which occur frequently in number theory and analysis, and Lovelace's diagram is considered the first computer program, more specifically, an execution trace algorithm. Execution traces are important tools for software developers because they provide insight into how their applications behave.

Work on the Difference Engine, beset with manufacturing and inter-personal problems, came to a standstill. But Babbage realized the potential of a more general computational approach: an Analytical Engine that could be programmed via Jacquard's punch card system. While never completed, its arithmetic logic, conditional control, and approach to integrated memory and programming would form the basic building blocks of the computers we know today. And while mar-ginalized in her time, Ada Lovelace can be seen today as the mother of (algorithmic) invention.

With the advantage of hindsight, Lovelace can also be claimed as an early figure in generative art with comments contained in a translator's note that would take more than a century and a half before being realized.

> *The operating mechanism can even be thrown into action independently of any object to operate upon (although of course no result could then be developed). Again, it might act upon other things besides number ... Supposing, for instance, that the fundamental relations of pitched sounds in the science of harmony and of musical composition were susceptible of such expression and adaptations, the engine might compose elaborate and scientific pieces of music of any degree of complexity or extent.* —Ada Lovelace[1]

Opposite: An image of Ada Lovelace, author of the first algorithm designed to be carried out by a machine, as rendered by a generative algorithm.

New Creative Paradigms

If an algorithm is a set of instructions, arranged in a specific order, for completing a task or solving a problem, then an intriguing starting point for our inquiry into AI and creativity would be two movements in art history: Dada and Surrealism.

The first World War was a technological moment when the forces of science, industry, and logic saw previously unimagined levels of destruction. Both the Dadaists and the Surrealists felt rational thought had brought humanity to that point. Dada tended to produce illogical work, made with non-traditional methods—collage, found objects, random actions—and an anti-establishment attitude.

The Surrealists saw the rationality of institutions and the established order as unresolved, in competition with, or contradictory to, the unconscious. Building on the techniques of Sigmund Freud's psychoanalysis—free association, for example—the surrealists developed a range of strategies for entering or unlocking the irrational dream state, with the most foundational being automatism. Automatism can be loosely described as unconscious actions which are captured or documented. For example, an "author" might sit with a piece of paper and allow words to flow without judgment, or somehow record everything spoken while in a relaxed state. Visual artists, like Jean (Hans) Arp, would affix pieces of cut-out paper that had randomly fallen onto a canvas. And the photographer Man Ray would place objects on a piece of photographic paper, expose it to light, and then develop the resulting print.

The goal was to create a super-reality, a *surreality*, which resolved the unconscious and the rational. Any output—regardless of media—was acceptable, as long as it accessed the unconscious.

For our purposes, let's consider Dada and Surrealism's aesthetic effect. This was a moment where "modern" artists like Alberto Giacometti and Pablo Picasso drew inspiration from the traditional art of Africa, Oceania, and "othered" populations. The colonization of these regions established cultural exchanges where the introduction of non-Western forms at first challenged, then began to expand the aesthetic taste of all forms of audiences. Repressed "primitive" nature began to emerge in paintings like Picasso's *Les Demoiselles d'Avignon* (1907) and Igor Stravinsky's orchestral work *Le Sacre du printemps (The Rite of Spring)* (1913). The id was reified and made consumable.

Opposite: An example of a Rayograph: Man Ray's technique of arranging objects on photographic paper, exposing them to light, and then developing the results.

For the rest of the twentieth century, art produced by unconscious means, indeterminacy, or non-intervention entered the aesthetic canon, where it remains to this day. In 1951, John Cage used the I Ching divination system as guidance in his *Music of Changes*, and 24 performers adjusting 12 radios as the instrumentation for *Imaginary Landscape No. 4 (March No. 2)*. After being introduced to the technique by poet and artist Brion Gysin, Beat writer William S. Burroughs popularized the cut-up. The first published appearance of cut-ups was *Minutes to Go*, a 1968 collection of texts by Burroughs, Gysin, Sinclair Beiles, and Gregory Corso. To make a cut-up, one took pages with text on it, cut it in halves or quarters, and then rearranged them to create new texts. The result produced surprising combinations, some of which, like "blade runner" or "heavy metal," have taken on significant cultural relevance.

An interesting side note about Burroughs is that his grandfather, William Seward Burroughs I, perfected the adding machine—his 1888 patent called it a "calculating machine." Along with the telephone and the filing cabinet, the adding machine can be considered a significant innovation of nineteenth-century information technology. Media historian Craig Robertson writes how our relation to information on paper—like that of the adding machine's output—changed at this moment: "Information, grasped as individual pieces of paper, became malleable, both in its physical shape and its contents."[2]

So far, we've focused on more hands-on conditions. With the electrification of devices, the relationship between input and output further distanced artist from output. The work produced shifted away from indices of the creator's hand such as the brush stroke or the breath. In 1920, Soviet physicist Leon Theremin, while engaged in government-sponsored research in proximity sensors, invented a new musical instrument that did not require physical contact with the performer. The Theremin consisted of two antennas which sensed the relative position of the performer's hands, one controlling pitch, the other volume. The resulting sound was otherworldly and once described by the *New York Times* music critic Harold C. Schonberg as "[a] cello lost in a dense fog, crying because it does not know how to get home."

The Theremin was sporadically used for the next few decades, notably for the soundtracks to Alfred Hitchcock's *Spellbound* (1945) and Robert Wise's *The Day the Earth Stood Still* (1951). But it was a notoriously difficult instrument to play, and thus remained a marginal instrument,

Opposite: John Cage composed music by applying the I Ching to randomly selected coins.

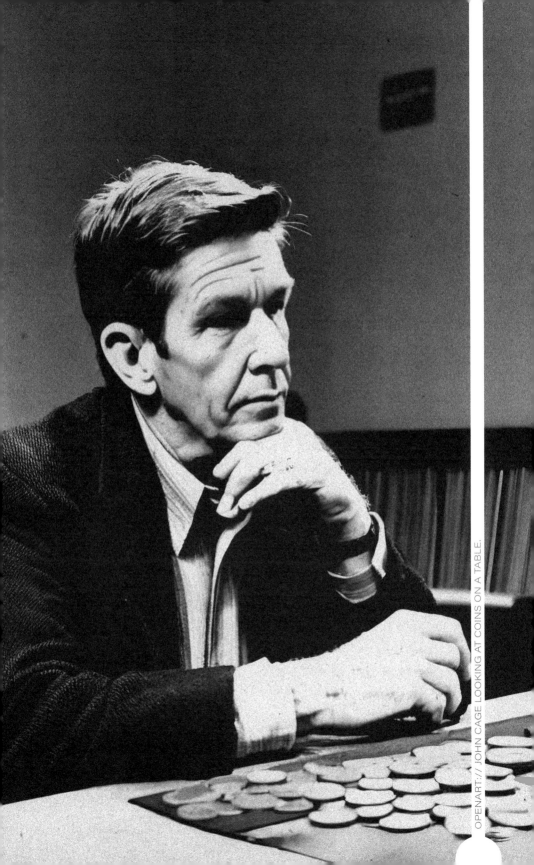

popular with hobbyists, until its resurgence after the 1993 premiere of the Steven M. Martin documentary *Theremin: An Electronic Odyssey*. While hard to play, Theremins were relatively easy to build. In 1964, Robert Moog, Theremin builder and Ph.D. candidate in engineering, introduced the first commercial analog synthesizer. Though it was sold without any guides or instruction, the synthesizer was comparatively easier to play than the Theremin because it had a piano-like keyboard. So aspects of traditional keyboard training were transferable. Instead of the piano mechanism where depressing a key caused tuned strings to be struck with hammers, synthesizer sounds began with oscillator-generated waveforms whose pitches and loudness were adjusted through changes in voltage.

Four years after its introduction, the Moog synthesizer was the featured instrument on Wendy Carlos's premiere album *Switched-On Bach*, which topped *Billboard* magazine's Classical Albums chart from 1969 to 1972, and became the second classical music album to be certified platinum, with more than one million units sold.

Since then, synthesizers continue to appear in all forms of music, in film and television soundtracks, and ringtones. And several digital Moog synthesizer apps are now available to the general public at a fraction of the cost, as well as generative art and music platforms designed by musician and visual artist Brian Eno in collaboration with musician and software designer Peter Chilvers.

Eno is a singular figure, a combination of provocateur and sage, who has continually been on the forefront of technology and experimentation, and not afraid to blend genres or traditions. After a brief role in the rock band Roxy Music, he began a solo career that ranged from traditional song form where every decision was intentionally made, to music where decisions were either abdicated or guided by someone or something else. Quite often, Eno would turn to his Oblique Strategies: a deck of 128 cards, each printed with a challenging constraint such as "Honor thy error as a hidden intention" or "Repetition is a form of change." The cards are used to break creative blocks by encouraging artists to shift their mode of thinking, step outside of their taste, or reject technical virtuosity, an approach very much in line with the Surrealists.

Eno also navigated around virtuosity through the systems he used in the studio. One widely-known technique was tape looping, where reel-to-reel tape containing recorded sound was spliced into a loop

Opposite: The theremin is a musical instrument that is played without being touched.

and played continuously. Eno placed two reel-to-reel machines side-by-side, with the spliced tape running from the one to the other. The output from one machine was recorded by the second onto the same tape, creating layers upon layers of sound. By adjusting the speed of the machines, Eno was able to create very slow, limpid pieces of music that were more environmental than melodic.

With the introduction of the compact disc, Eno was able to increase the number of outputs and randomness by recording a variety of loops, all at different time occurrences, and then playing each on a separate player. The piece would theoretically run for decades before any pattern would repeat. And in 1995, Eno began to work with SSEYO's (now known as Intermorphic) generative music software, Koan. The system generated ever-changing music where the only "composing" on Eno's part consisted of tonal inputs and general parameters, thus affirming the suppositions of Ada Lovelace's translator's note.

One doesn't necessarily listen to this kind of music like one listens in concert or a club. Eno would set up dark environments where audiences could come and go as they please, spend time on a sofa, and view light pieces which slowly changed color in the same randomized manner as the music. Today, instead of traveling to an installation, audiences can purchase digital pieces that generate a similar effect and play it back on their home system, with almost infinite variations, for as long as they like.

The automatism of the Surrealists, the indeterminacy of John Cage, and the cut-ups of William S. Burroughs, combined with the technological descendants of Leon Theremin and Robert Moog, all run through Eno's work. And while it sounds avant-garde, Eno is the farthest thing from an obscure figure. He has produced and collaborated with the biggest acts, including David Bowie, U2, Coldplay, and The Talking Heads, and composed the Microsoft Windows startup tone. What was once aesthetically-challenging no longer looks or sounds foreign. In fact, much of Eno's experimental work feels very human and approachable. Its narrative is really only about its making, which makes it easier for the audience to project their own subjective associations onto the experience. And after a century and a half of modernist experimentation, we have the ability to quickly understand pretty much any aesthetic phenomena.

Opposite: Tape loops are made by running audio tape across two reel-to-reel machines. Overdubbing onto the existing loop allows for a gradual sonic layering often heard in contemporary music.

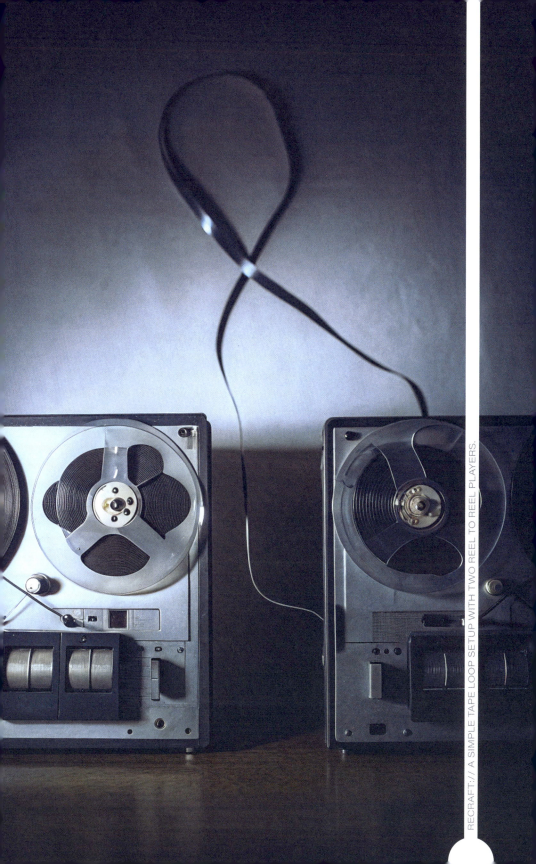

It is simple human nature for the strange to eventually become familiar, but we do live in a time when it feels like anything we desire can be manifested. And with the panoply of stories and narratives readily available on any streaming platform, the conduit to our dreams and wishes has never been more accessible, nor more capable to be customized to our specifications. Where the Surrealists had to purposely create the conditions for automatism, we surf across platforms, almost unconsciously, until something tickles our fancy. No special techniques or processes required. It is a different kind of free association, a different kind of algorithm—to use our broad definition. As brand consultant and clinical psychologist Dr. Tom Guarriello writes in *The Meaning of Branded Objects*, "Fulfilling my secret wishes will increasingly become a basic expectation for brands to provide "good customer service."[3]

Carl Jung was an early follower of Freud, who later parted ways and developed analytical psychology, a system separate from psychoanalysis. In Jungian theory, the "collective unconscious" represents that part of the mind containing memories and impulses of which the individual is not aware. These memories and impulses, which originate in the structure of the brain, are common across all of humanity in the form of archetypes, symbols, and instincts. Since we know how current algorithms on social media and streaming services tend to push audiences to the middle, the question now becomes how authentic our dreams really are.

There is a haunting line in Toni Morrison's *Playing in the Dark* that sums up the potential capacity for wish fulfillment in the age of AI: "I came to realize the obvious: the subject of the dream is the dreamer."[4]

The Soulless Apparition

Much of the anxiety directed toward AI most likely comes from a fear of animated anthropomorphic beings that are uncontrollable. Stories of such entities, known as golems, are found in early Judaism. To make a golem, inert matter, such as clay or mud, is formed into the shape of a man. The form is then ritualistically brought to life as a mystical incantation is written on a piece of paper, and then inserted into the being's mouth. Today, we would say that the golem was programmed.

Opposite: The application of AI by brands can approach the fulfillment of customer dreams; the subject of which is the customer themself.

Combined with the human tendency to anthropomorphize, pretty much any man-made object has potential to become golem-esque. The robot vacuum creeping along your wall, then bumping repeatedly into your foot only looks cute because you're projecting a sense of subjectivity onto it. And at the same time, your pet runs away from it because they're projecting their own subjectivity onto the same object. The robot vacuum is, at the same time, harmlessly dumb and threateningly uncontrollable.

Around the time of Jacquard and Babbage, a group of English textile workers were concerned about the effect of automation on their livelihoods and quality of life. Calling themselves the Luddites—after the legendary weaver Ned Ludd—they organized raiding parties to destroy the new technology, staged public demonstrations, and engaged in letter-writing campaigns to petition government officials. When the Luddites began to kidnap and assassinate mill owners, the government stepped in with equally violent results.

Today, the term "Luddite" has come to mean anyone opposing or resisting new technologies. And like the original Luddites, the fear of financial displacement remains a common motivation. But along with the desire to control productivity and maximize output, as displayed by Jacquard and Babbage, digital technology introduced a kind of threat where the stakes felt different ... disembodied.

Beginning in 1949, a group of British scientists and intellectuals calling themselves The Ratio Club gathered regularly to discuss cybernetics: an interdisciplinary field dealing with control and communication in both animals and machines. The initial focus of cybernetics was the seeming similarities in both biological and technological situations known as circular causality. In such a sequence, the effect of an action elicits a response that leads back to the original action and creates a feedback loop. For example, in family dynamics, circular causality describes why one person's anger causes another to withdraw, and how that withdrawal sparks further anger from the first. In technology, circular causality describes how a thermometer maintains a consistent temperature. Causal reasoning in machine learning is an important area of research which may have implications across a wide variety of fields. One of the members of the Ratio Club was a brilliant theoretical

Opposite: Cybernetics is thought of as the merging of humans and technology à la cyborgs, etc. But it is simply the study of control, feedback, and communication. A simple example is the interaction of sailor and boat.

mathematician named Alan Turing. During the war, Turing played a crucial role in British efforts to decode German navy communications. Their electromechanical cipher machine, known as Enigma, was considered to generate extremely secure messages that were unbreakable, unless one had a matching machine and the secret key list for the day. Along with a fellow code-breaker, Turing invented a machine known as the Bombe that significantly sped up the code-breaking work.

Turing was one of the first to give considerable thought to machine intelligence. Before his codebreaking work, he had previously conceived a hypothetical computing device capable of modifying or improving its own program. In a 1947 lecture to the London Mathematical Society, Turing was perhaps the first to publicly use the term "computer intelligence" as he described how such machines might work, in support of human activity, and what would be needed for that to happen: "What we want is a machine that can learn from experience."

If one has an intelligent computer, how would one determine if it was intelligent? Turing devised a test where a human judge asked natural language questions to another human and a computer. The conversations would be in writing via computer terminals to disguise their origin, and the goal would not be to give correct answers, but rather mimic the kind of answers a human might give. Turing introduced the test in his 1950 journal article "Computing Machinery and Intelligence," which had the famous opening line "I propose to consider the question, 'Can machines think?'"[5]

But what would be the nature of that thinking? American psychologist and computer scientist J. C. R. Licklider published a paper in 1960 titled "Man-Computer Symbiosis," which laid out his vision of a complementary relationship that leveraged the inherent strengths of both. Licklider saw the aim of such a symbiosis to be twofold. First off was "bring[ing] the computing machine effectively into the formative parts of technical problems," and the second was "bring[ing] computing machines effectively into processes of thinking that must go on in 'real time,' time that moves too fast to permit using computers in conventional ways." He then offers a situation where such real-time responsiveness would be ideal: in battle. Of course such a symbiosis would "require much tighter coupling between man and machine than is ... possible today."[6]

Opposite: Alan Turing devised an early test to determine the presence of computer intelligence.

In 1962, Licklider was appointed head of the Information Processing Techniques Office at the United States Department of Defense Advanced Research Projects Agency (ARPA, later known as DARPA). While more of an idea man than an inventor, he made three significant contributions to the growing field of information technology: the institution of computer science departments in major universities, the concept of time-sharing, and networked computers. Computer science departments would supply the growing need for trained engineers and programmers, time-sharing addressed the current high expense of owning and running computer equipment, and a network of computers, as described in his memorandum addressed to "Members and Affiliates of the Intergalactic Computer Network," was "an electronic commons open to all."

Two and a half decades later, Licklider's proposed network became reality when Tim Berners-Lee invented the HTML (Hypertext Markup Language), the URL (Uniform Resource Locator) web address system, HTTP (Hypertext Transfer Protocol), and posted the first website. And a quick look around at people and their devices might suggest that Licklider's "tighter coupling between man and machine" is moving along as imagined. The line between the biological and the technological is quite blurry. No longer do we need to remember phone numbers, do math in our head, or remember the best route to a nearby city. We offload our memories to our devices, they do the math for us, and they tell us where to turn.

That overlap—into the realm of cybernetic organisms, or cyborgs—where flesh and machine are completely united is the territory where algorithms translate the physical world into the digital. The physical world is immensely complex and dynamic, and as Licklider pointed out, one cannot code everything beforehand—a condition mathematicians call "combinatorial explosion." Any computational response needs to be in real time and capable of adjusting to dynamic conditions. Which is why it is so difficult to create accurate long-range weather forecasts.

Nature stands as a model of a system able to operate in real time—capable of receiving inputs, transferring impulses, analyzing data, and self-correction—in biological nervous systems. So an obvious first step would be to model individual neurons and then arrange them into a nonlinear neural network. In nonlinear systems, the output is not directly proportional to the input, like in the linear equation $x=y^2$.

Opposite: A diagram of a basic nonlinear neural network. Each node represents a single computational cell, known as a neuron.

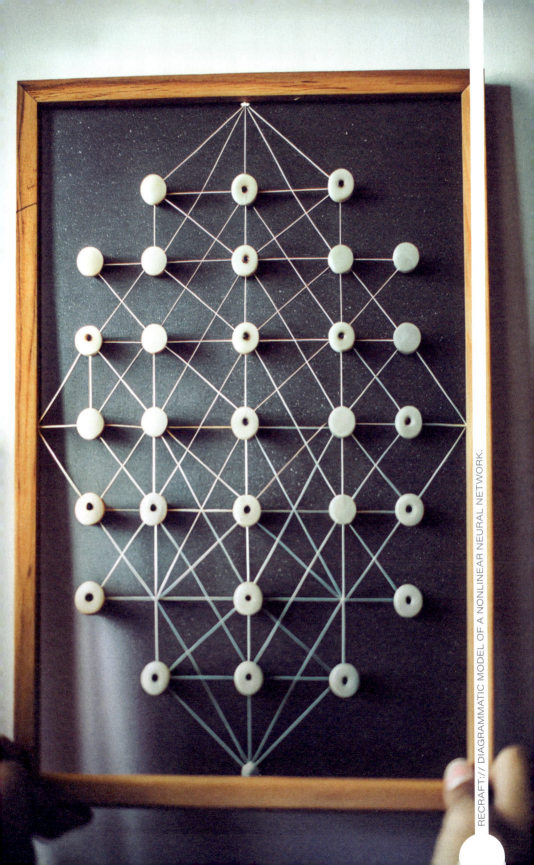

For any number x, there is a number that, when squared, will solve that equation. And from there, we can build mathematical theories which define aspects of much more dynamic systems, but only aspects— again, the problem of long-range weather forecasts. This is where the ability to self-correct after incorrect output is desirable.

In July 1958, Frank Rosenblatt, a research psychologist and engineer at the Cornell Aeronautical Laboratory in Buffalo, New York, fed into a room-size IBM computer a series of punch cards—descendants of Jacquard's invention. After 50 trials, the computer taught itself to distinguish between cards marked on the left from cards marked on the right. Rosenblatt had applied a mathematical model, or algorithm, known as a "perceptron." The perceptron imitates the biological neuron in the simplest manner by receiving binary inputs (on/off, yes/no) and producing a binary output. Beginning with a statistical model that had been trained with inputs—in Rosenblatt's case, the punch cards— and desired outputs (left versus right), the perceptron could map new data to the expected output. An ideal algorithm would have the ability to generalize from its training and generate *reasonably* accurate outputs for unseen circumstances.

Rosenblatt had demonstrated the first application of a hypothesis, offered a decade earlier by neuroscientist Warren McCulloch and logician Walter Pitts, that the human mind's capacity for logical thought was a direct result of neurons that themselves performed logical operations. This conceptual turning point set the path for todays' work in AI and is where computational theories of consciousness are derived. Basically, Rosenblatt had built a machine that could, for all intents and purposes, think, in the most basic definition of the term.

Two years later, Rosenblatt's Mark I Perceptron connected a "retina" of 400 photocells to a set of association neurons, which then determined whether an image shown was pointing up or down, the letter C or a triangle, or any other taught set of outputs. The thickness and design of the input shapes were significant because if they were not heavy nor distinct enough, the crude perception of the retina would not be able to establish a distinctive input—a problem which persists today when vision-based AI is used on darker skin or in low-light conditions.

Opposite top: Frank Rosenblatt at the Mark I Perceptron, 1960.

Opposite bottom: The Perceptron "learning" to discriminate the shapes of characters, 1961.

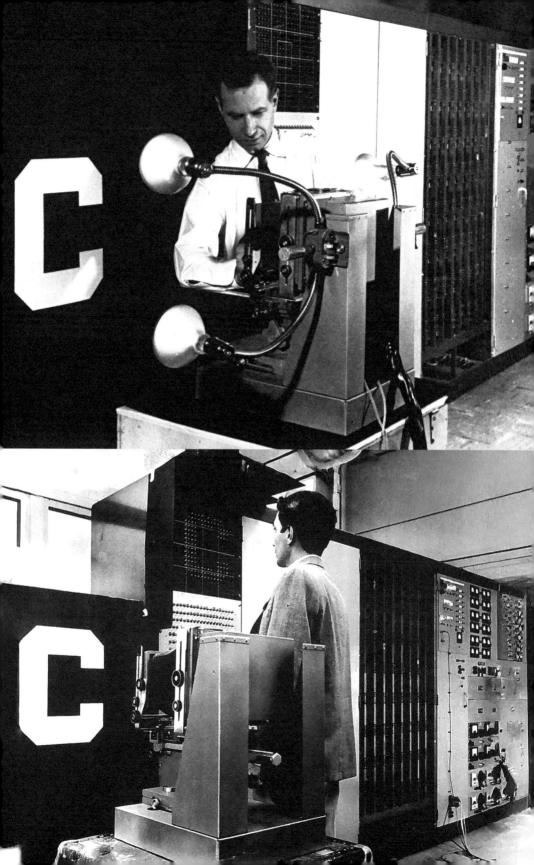

Rosenblatt was working on a grant from the Office of Naval Research at the time, and it was the Navy who organized the initial press conference in 1958. Compared to other breakthroughs at the time, news of the Perceptron attracted almost as much media hype as current developments in AI. A July 8, 1958 article in the *New York Times* with the headline "New Navy Device Learns By Doing" began: "The Navy revealed the embryo of an electronic computer today that it expects will be able to walk, talk, see, write, reproduce itself and be conscious of its existence." And further adding to the sci-fi futuristic hype, the article went on to say: "Perceptrons might be fired to the planets as mechanical space explorers ... Later Perceptrons will be able to recognize people and call out their names and instantly translate speech in one language to ... another."

Of course, such hype would attract critics. Rosenblatt's Perceptron was the most basic, minimum viable product of a neural net, only one layer deep. And that limitation formed the basis of *Perceptrons*, written by computer scientists Marvin Minsky and Seymour Papert. Minsky and Rosenblatt attended the same high school, and though very vocal in their public disagreements, remained on cordial terms. *Perceptrons* proved mathematically that a single-layer neural net was limited in what discriminations it could perform.

The mid-twentieth century was an exuberant time for the nascent AI field, and the consensus was machine intelligence would emerge in just a few years. Years of intellectual and engineering breakthroughs attracted increasing amounts of government funding and fueled an expanding field of interdisciplinary research. As Licklider identified, there was a need for more university departments where mathematicians, engineers, programmers, psychologists, and even philosophers could collaborate.

But eventually, all hype cycles lead to cycles of retrenchment, and the slow progress of AI research, combined with Minsky and Papert's book, led to what has come to be known as the AI Winter. In the United States, DARPA cancelled or cut AI funding in favor of other pursuits, and in the United Kingdom, AI research was derided as led by charlatans and depleting resources better deployed elsewhere. An influential article by British mathematician James Lighthill identified the widespread disappointment of AI research workers in the overpromises and underachievements of the previous twenty-five years.[7]

But over the next decade, as computers became more affordable and integrated into businesses, AI research turned to the application of inference engines to knowledge bases. Inference engines use logic that follows IF-THEN rules, a powerful logic mechanism which greatly reduces computational resources because it avoids the kind of procedural programming that would take much longer to resolve. Applying inference engines to specific knowledge bases simulates the kind of decision making one would receive from a human expert.

The earliest "expert systems" as they were called, avoided uncertainty by using strict logical reasoning. But that is impractical in the real world. So subsequent systems were built with probabilistic techniques, and later on, rule-based approaches which added a bit of leeway to accommodate uncertainty.

Expert systems in business use caught on rather quickly. The first commercial AI product, an expert system, arrived at Digital Equipment Corporation (DEC) in the early 1980s. The program implemented business rules to automate routine and repetitive tasks and was used to help configure orders for new computer systems—echoes of the Perceptron's promise of reproduction. By 1986 it was estimated to have saved DEC $40 million a year. This experiment caught the attention of many companies, and a new industry was born.

Numerous information and technology companies introduced expert systems products to businesses, designing their own proprietary solutions intended to help everything from medical diagnoses, to financial decisions, to oil exploration. But designing for complex problems comes with a matching complexity in customization, requiring the additional costs of research and planning, followed by slow implementation, debugging, and training. And while the stand-alone expert systems industry was short-lived, the technology remains embedded in many contemporary solutions, most of which are built upon the scaffolding of earlier systems but minus any specific customizations.

The result is a creeping push of process and benchmarks toward a common middle due to behavioral momentum and the overwhelming volume of data produced every day. As the brief moment in human history in which one has a job for life recedes into the past, new hires now tend to be vetted against their conformity to preexisting skills and their ability to jump in as fully-capable team members.

And with the application of big data to identify new opportunities, and make better decisions and predictions, companies have turned data analytics to their employees. Human resources management systems and people analytics allow for employees to be defined in terms of their data. And that abstraction turns people into interchangeable objects, under more surveillance, with less privacy, less job security, and more bureaucracy.

A prominent theme in Karl Marx is the estrangement of people from their work, their human nature, and ultimately their selves. He saw how the division of labor in a capitalist society, where people live as mechanistic parts of a working class, resulted in feelings of alienation—compounded today with the rise of contract work and employee churn. The *Grundrisse*, published after Marx's death, pulls a quote from the Welsh reformer Robert Owen, a leading figure of the Industrial Revolution in the development of socialist economic thought, and founder of the cooperative movement:

> *Since the general introduction of inanimate mechanism into British manufactories, man, with few exceptions, has been treated as a secondary and inferior machine; and far more attention has been given to perfect the raw materials of wood and metals than those of body and mind. Give but due reflection to the subject, and you will find that man, even as an instrument for the creation of wealth, may be still greatly improved.* — Robert Owen[8]

Interestingly, Marx's English translators use the word "soulless" in place of the original "inanimate." Encountering the soulless places us in "the uncanny valley," the term to describe the discomfort or unease upon experiencing something that looks alive, but is not fully convincing. Examples would be human-looking robots, the quadrupedal robots created by Boston Dynamics, and the digitally-created version of the actor Peter Cushing—who passed away in 1994—in the 2016 film *Rogue One: A Star Wars Story*.

Research on the uncanny valley suggests that the feeling disappears when the object in question does something useful, which is why we are not creeped out by a robot vacuum, but our pets are. To us, it removes a chore, while the family dog sees it as an uncontrollable entity. And perhaps that is partially why the last century of reducing biological and mental systems to the level of simple machines—artificial neurons, mechanical vision, decision making—does not freak us out as much. It happened so gradually and showed its value relatively quickly. And it was the result of calculative thinking, with each logical step directed toward a positive goal of an idealized future state.

To go against the digital tide is difficult. Looking back on the last two centuries of effort spent developing the machines, devices, and algorithms which embody our hopes for growth and profit, it is

---

Opposite: The "uncanny" feeling disappears when an autonomous object does something useful.

understandable why we perceive a certain elegance to it all. And understandable why we accommodate the speed and demands of this system. Because technology is a reframing, we are unable to see the knock-on effects of efficiencies and wonders as they debut. All we can do is look to history, which helps when considering human behavior, but is inadequate to fully capture the wake of our machinery.

AI as a Brand

Untangling the brand phenomena "AI" from the thing itself requires a degree of discipline. Because above all, AI is a marketing tool. Yes, it is the toolset used to analyze markets, track customers, create advertising, deliver services, and thousands of other applications. But it is also a phrase marketers and advertisers use to evoke any number of associations.

Perhaps one can point to November 30, 2022, when OpenAI released an early demo of ChatGPT, as the beginning of a generative AI mania. Within five days, it had gone viral on social media and gained more than one million users. And within two months, it surpassed 100 million users, making it the fastest-growing consumer software application in history. Compared to other software, the learning curve was relatively flat. A beginner could "generate" a passable poem, recipe, or text almost immediately. On closer inspection, the text was most likely drivel, but wasn't most of the text that society generated equally as vacuous?

OpenAI, the company behind ChatGPT was founded in 2015, and had previously launched the DALL-E text-to-image platform. Chat and DALL-E, both distant descendants of expert systems, were built upon large language models that were trained on large amounts of text data that generally came from the Internet. Because algorithms process numbers rather than text, all text used in both platforms has to be tokenized. This is a process where unique integers are arbitrarily assigned to each vocabulary entry and embedded into a representation of a word, a sentence, or eventually a document.

Opposite: An example of the ChatGPT 2.0 tokenization process. Note how the results are filtered towards semantics (punctuation, capitalization, spaces, etc.) and not meaning.

Text to be tokenized

My dog's name is Tula.
Mon chien s'appelle Tula.

20 tokens produced

3666 3290 338 1438 318 309 4712 13 198
9069 442 2013 264 6 1324 13485 309 4712 13 198

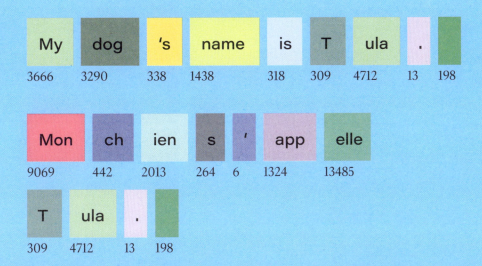

Even though tokenization is more computationally efficient than using natural language, generative platforms still require an immense amount of money and energy in training and server costs ... as well as all the input data stolen from every artist, writer, and musician foolish enough to upload their work on the Internet. Still, to the average user, the magic of instant creation is captivating. The power of databases and algorithms is too abstract for most. The language quickly slips into mathematical equations, anagrams, and industry jargon. (What's a GPT anyway?)

But a picture or an instant love letter, well that's immediate. Feelings can come to life. Immediately.

The general public now had something they could hold in their minds whenever they heard the word "AI." And combined with the breathtaking amounts of money associated with any company that owned a platform, supplied a computer chip, or held a patent, AI was now a speculative market.

One of the more egregious patterns of an AI-as-marketing tool is the parade of agencies, consultancies, marketers, and brand builders all scrambling for market position or supremacy. Microsoft Advertising tracked a 566 percent volume increase from 2022 to 2023 in AI-related search terms, which means that if the general public is interested, then the marketing community is obsessed. Any chance to build AI-features into products is actively pursued, producing refrigerators that can design recipes, or "copilots" that go beyond word prompting and actually write the email for you. The result is that as of the second quarter of 2024, only 29 percent of respondents to a survey by the Lippincott brand agency felt that their experience with AI lived up to expectations. The same survey indicated only a third of respondents sustained any sense of curiosity about AI in the future, with more expressing skepticism.

Perhaps it is because AI as a widely distributed consumer product suffers from poor performance. Apple's digital assistant Siri is a source of constant frustration and errors, and Microsoft's assistant, Copilot for Microsoft 365, promised "thousands of skills" and "infinite possibilities for enterprise," yet the infinite possibilities it offered included summarizing emails and querying Excel spreadsheets. The output of generative AI is still on a steep learning curve. It continues to "hallucinate" nonexistent patterns or objects which then lead to nonsensical or just plain incorrect outputs, and word embeddings may perpetuate biases and stereotypes contained in the trained dataset.

The current state of generative AI does not fully solve the complex problems that are presented to it. The tokenized strings of text are run through probability models, which are then purposely formed into answers. It does not know anything in the way we know things—through experience or reasoning—it just generates output in a form that we understand to be answers. That may pass in a business environment built on professional expectations which are often performative, but is it truly a solution?

This inability to produce business-critical solutions is probably why a year after Copilot debuted, a CNBC survey revealed that 50 percent of respondents said their organizations had deployed the tech to all employees, another 17 percent say they decided not to fully adopt Copilot, and another third of companies remain in the testing phase. Then when asked whether the $30 monthly per user for Copilot was worth the cost, many were not sure.

These are underwhelming results, and not much business value, for an industry that spent upwards of $200 billion to expand data centers in 2024, which was 50 percent more than in 2023. On a June 2024 podcast, Dario Amodei, the co-founder and CEO of Anthropic—a competitor to OpenAI and the company behind Claude AI, another platform like ChatGPT—said the cost to train an AI model was then $1 billion, and was anticipated to rise over the subsequent three years to anywhere from $10 billion to $100 billion. This tracks with the history of ChatGPT. Version 2.0, released in 2019, cost $40,000 to train; version 3.0 from 2020 cost $4.5 million; 2023's version 4.0 release cost $100 million; and the work on version 5.0 is estimated to range from $1.25 billion to $2.25 billion.

This does not fully take into consideration all the obvious computing costs, including storage, data centers, networking equipment and services, the energy to run it all, and all the ancillary costs such as data labeling, model customization, security, and compliance. It may exist in the virtual, but the abilities of Large Language Models, which are the core of generative AI, remain tied to physical scale. The more a company spends on servers, infrastructure, and development, the greater the chances of building a successful product, which puts the entry costs out of reach to any but the largest corporations. Still, most companies envision a potential for generative AI to make the usage of computer, energy, and human resources more efficient.

The market has yet to determine whether OpenAI's o3 GPT model or DeepSeek-V3 will adequately address the hallucinating outputs or the financial barriers to input training. OpenAI taught their o3 model with "deliberative alignment," as part of a wider industry effort to build systems able to reason through complex tasks via extensive trial and error. The models then use that experience to evaluate techniques that lead to correct answers against ones that do not (echoes of Lovelace's execution trace). By repeating that process, it can begin to identify patterns. But still, it is based on the same core technology as the original hallucinating ChatGPT.

DeepSeek was developed in China after the American and European governments passed versions of their CHIPS Act. The legislation increased funding for semiconductor production in each region, reducing potential supply-chain exposure and regulating the export of graphics chips known as GPUs (graphics processing units). Because rendering images for video games and computer graphics is so computationally complex, GPUs became a crucial component for AI. In response to GPU shortages, Chinese programmers devised workarounds which distributed machine learning across networks, a technique known as "mixture of experts," which allowed DeepSeek to be trained for just over $5.5 million.

DeepSeek and o3 are the most recent examples of the basic truism that there will always be someone able to do it cheaper, better, more efficiently, and more accurately. But all of this concerns deep-pocketed companies with the temerity to remain in the economic, political, and social fray. As a product, brands, branding professionals, and marketers are all more excited about AI than the average customer.

When the average layperson thinks about AI, they easily tap into the collective consciousness of myths and narratives shared over generations of storytelling. While zombies and vampires are most likely not real, we know how to dispatch them in case they are. And we know what to look out for when confronted by a soulless apparition powered by artificial intelligence.

First is the recognition that they are misaligned with most human beings. Mary Shelley's 1818 novel *Frankenstein: or, The Modern Prometheus*, introduced a character—later called a demon by his creator, Victor Frankenstein—who realized immediately upon creation that his creator could not stand the sight of him. While taking care to select the most beautiful and well-proportioned body parts, a different emotion came over Frankenstein immediately.

Opposite: Victor Frankenstein's creation exemplifies our collective fears of soulless apparitions.

Oh! No mortal could support the horror of that countenance. A mummy again endued with animation could not be so hideous as that wretch. I had gazed on him while unfinished; he was ugly then, but when those muscles and joints were rendered capable of motion, it became a thing such as even Dante could not have conceived. —Mary Shelley

And upon seeing his reflection, the demon was also repulsed. Later in the story, out of a desire to find love and acceptance, he asked Frankenstein to create a companion. Frankenstein initially agreed, but destroyed the second creation out of fear of establishing a race of monsters, a fear that resonates with the anxiety of the historical Luddites—a nonhuman creation out of sync with society.

Another connection resonates in the subtitle of Shelley's book: *The Modern Prometheus*. In Greek mythology, Prometheus was the figure who brought fire to humanity, against the wishes of the gods. For our usage, fire can be seen as a metaphor for knowledge or technology, but it is not a cautionary tale. Prometheus acted out of love and admiration for humanity, and the gift of fire was the gift of civilization. This time, a nonhuman benefactor creating society.

It is this tension that vibrates throughout the brand of AI, and pretty much every technology brand as well. And the myths go back more than two millennia. For every *Sorcerer's Apprentice* (both the version by Goethe and by Disney), there is the tale of Pygmalion and his creation Galatea. For every Terminator, there is Commander Data from *Star Trek: The Next Generation*. For every HAL 9000 from *2001: A Space Odyssey*, there is *Iron Man*'s Jarvis.

Each of these figures reveals something about the world and ourselves, as did artists such as the Surrealists, William S. Burroughs, and Brian Eno. And the same could be said for the innovations of Jacquard, Babbage, Turing, and Rosenblatt. AI is a recruitment strategy that channels the forces of efficiency, creativity, and automation through society; and our relationship with time, thought, work, the unconscious, and the stories we tell ourselves have all changed forever. Before AI, trees were trees and mountains were mountains. As we grapple with AI, trees are no longer trees and mountains are no longer mountains. Once AI becomes reliable and as normalized as personal computers are today, trees will once again be trees and mountains will be mountains.

Innovation can alienate because established materials and processes are transformed, disappear, or are taken away. "The way we've always done things" is comfortable, but it does not look forward. Henry Ford is falsely quoted as saying: "If I had asked people what they wanted, they would have said faster horses." In reality, he said: "If there is any one secret of success, it lies in the ability to get the other person's point of view and see things from that person's angle as well as from your own." Regardless of his social viewpoints, that may be the essence of branding, and another way to describe seeing others as subjects, and not as objects.

1   Craig Robertson, "Granular Certainty, the Vertical Filing Cabinet, and the Transformation of Files," in *Administory* (December 2019).

2   Ada Lovelace, "Notes by the Translator," in Note A, L. F. Menabrea, *Sketch of the Analytical Engine Invented by Charles Babbage*, originally published in French in the *Bibliothèque Universelle de Genève* (October 1842, No. 82).

3   Tom Guarriello, Ph.D., *The Meaning of Branded Objects* (Rockport, 2025).

4   Toni Morrison, *Playing in the Dark: Whiteness and the Literary Imagination* (Vintage Books, 1993).

5   Alan Turing, "Computing Machinery and Intelligence," in October 1950, *Mind*, volume LIX, issue 236 (October 1950).

6   J. C. R. Licklider, "Man-Computer Symbiosis," in *IRE Transactions on Human Factors in Electronics*, volume HFE-1 (March 1960)

7   James Lighthill, "Artificial Intelligence: A General Survey," in *Artificial Intelligence: A Paper Symposium* (UK: Science Research Council, 1973).

8   Robert Owen, *Essays on the Formation of the Human Character* (London, 1840).

Clerk, Colleague, Coach, Tarot Reader?

Now that we have some foundation into the nature of intelligence and consciousness, and have explored the brand history of AI, we will eventually have to roll up our sleeves and use this new tool.

That is the first problem.

Because in a sense, there are no tools, and ... everything is a tool. If one has an AI platform on their smartphone, then the interface is nothing more than a text chain. If one is a graphic designer, then the interface is a dialog box in Photoshop. Or, worse yet, you are creating professional work in Canva, a program you used to think was only for amateurs.

The instrumentality of our favorite tools is changing, and might possibly disappear altogether. Given the recent trend of software moving to a subscription program, there is an inevitable logic to that. Generative platforms like ChatGPT or Midjourney have always been web-based.

And there is an anthropological disconnect to that because for the longest time, our tools always had a physical presence. We picked them up, swung them around, and took care of them. Our bodies learned how they behaved in the world, taking in consideration the effects of gravity and friction. Then when the computer entered our lives, we still had a degree of control with our tools, but our physical connection was distanced. There were material issues of speed, storage, and capacity, but these were conceptual connections instead of corporeal. Still, in both modalities, we think with objects. We engage in material thinking. In other words, the friction of creation—hammering a nail, waiting for paint to dry, adding an adjustment layer to an image, running a document through spell check, hitting Command-Z—affects how we think about our work. Somehow, it connects us to the process, thus situating us in time and space.

AI brings us to a different place. When we enter a prompt, we are engaging not in material thinking, but in *representational thinking*. This is a frictionless, positive space programmed to supply outputs that are offered up as answers. We have to continually ask ourselves if we are actively thinking through the problem instead of passively receiving responses.

Otherwise we are just a conductor.

Personas

Oftentimes, more successful brands convey a certain character, as in an actual persona. We know how someone in Converse sneakers differs from someone in Timberland boots in a broad sense. And if the person in Converse is also in a Prada jacket, and the Timberlands are paired with a North Face parka, the character of each comes more into focus.

We previously saw how AI can convey a variety of characteristic associations, but that is relegated to the consumption of the brand, and not how one might *work with* some form of AI. How might we establish a material relationship?

AI is the commodity that launched a thousand podcasts, and unfortunately, most of the material is noise. But in 2024, the scientist and author Andrew McAfee appeared on a couple of podcasts and offered an intriguing proposal: a way to find an appropriate role or application for AI is to treat it as either a clerk, a colleague, or a coach. It is an elegant approach that helps frame a working relationship.

Clerk

This is the "low-hanging fruit" of AI, and a function that has been with us for some time (Microsoft Office 97 introduced "Clippy," a paper clip-shaped character designed to assist users). And admittedly, this is also where the displacement of workers hits hard.

Opposite: "Clippy" was the nickname given to the animated paperclip character that served as a virtual assistant in early versions of Microsoft Office.

Over the last couple of decades, branding and advertising firms have experienced contraction. Larger clients are bringing their branding work in-house; programmatic media buying offers cost savings, precision targeting, and enhanced personalization; and holding-company shareholders continue to expect returns. No client today could be blamed for questioning an agency's invoice for a task that was probably completed with the help of an AI. And in response, many strategy departments across branding and advertising have been decimated.

Granted, pretty much every job has a task or two that is repetitive, time-consuming, competes for attention better directed to higher-order activities, or is just plain dull. Transcribing conversations, reviewing documents, and reordering data are the kind of tasks that are perfect opportunities for an AI "clerk" to cover.

One might want to take a moment and evaluate the cultural effects of AI in this situation.

For a smaller organization, or a lean staff, repetitive and time-consuming tasks should probably be done by an AI because they eat into productivity. But reliance on AI in a distinctly unique company culture or sector may be educationally harmful.

Entry-level employees typically learn higher-order skills through foundational tasks such as gathering data and updating presentation charts, especially if they are under the supervision of more senior staff. But as AI takes over these tasks, the opportunity to gain domain knowledge and learn from their supervisors disappears. If that foundational experience is lost, how will junior employees acquire the knowledge and experience so they might effectively check AI outputs? How would they even know what to ask for?

In a more specific example, junior law associates and paralegals were historically tasked with reviewing documents, organizing case files, legal research, and numerous other time-consuming tasks. The work was time-intensive and not glamorous, but it did expose younger employees to the nuances of the legal profession, offered a view into the social and professional requirements that come from experience, and helped build their professional network. Producing legal briefs for supervising attorneys also offered practical experience. There is a certain way in which lawyers look at the world that has been acquired through the junior associate experience. These skills are nontechnical,

Opposite: Transcribing, filing, and reordering are ideal tasks for an AI "clerk."

yet the introduction of AI into that equation changes that apprenticeship-like culture of education.

Weighing the benefits of AI is a difficult balance for the legal profession. On one hand, it reduces litigation costs and affords access to clients with limited means. On the other, using AI exposes privileged information to the large language models (LLMs) that fuel generative AI platforms, which creates confidentiality and intellectual property issues. Predictive AI can assist judges in issuing sentences—determining the probability of a guilty defendant's future actions—and it can perpetuate the inherent biases of the platform's encoding.

One can only imagine the complications across other industries.

Colleague

Many of us already have years of experience with AI "colleagues." If you have ever flowed text into Google Translate or used an Instagram filter, then you have, in a sense, collaborated with an AI by asking it to transform something into something else. And if you are a designer, illustrator, art director, writer, or any other flavor of creative, take care that a simple transformation may fulfill the brief, but it may not be exceptional.

The American artist Jasper Johns has an equation for turning the familiar into the highest form of art: "Take an object. Do something to it. Do something else to it." Because generative AI is predictive, there is an inherent push to the familiar or expected. So doing "something else to it" is a step in a good direction.

Generative platforms are ideal as ideation tools. One can visualize an environment, run through alternative angles, or simply jumpstart things when the muse is absent. Abundant options can flow within minutes, and the creator then becomes editor or curator. But keep in mind that the level of finish can be so enchanting and perfect that it might be accepted too quickly. This is where a critical eye focused on the aesthetic, strategic, and narrative aspects of the output should be applied.

Opposite: AI "colleagues" are reading x-rays with increasing accuracy.

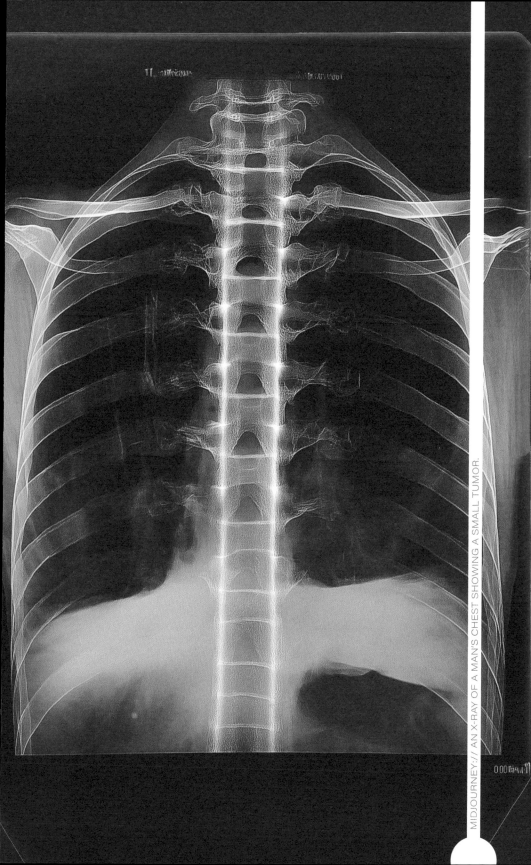

The colleague role does overlap with the clerk. For example, in a market analysis, an AI would probably be better at pattern recognition than a human. As it is when analyzing x-rays for medical diagnoses, or pinpointing areas with potential mineral deposits using satellite imagery.

Another potential overlap would be to use an AI agent as an interviewer in qualitative research. There are instances where a respondent might be reticent to disclose personal information, possibly medical or sexual histories, drug usage, or any previous legal troubles. Using an impersonal interviewer could remove the sort of self-editing one might engage in when speaking with another person.

Coach

Many of us have also worked with AI coaches, often in an annoying capacity. Every unwelcome chatbot that pops up on a website is a lesser version. This is where something like Copilot for Microsoft 365 was intended to improve upon, but as discussed previously, it continues to be met with resistance from companies and employees.

As AI clerks replace entry-level positions, there has also been growth in AI-powered knowledge management tools. Company knowledge is organized, stored, and presented with personalized recommendations for each employee, in response to previous behavior or individual needs. Surveys from the International Data Corporation (IDC) report that companies that have figured out how to use knowledge management have seen better decision making, improved customer support, increased customer and employee satisfaction, and improved employee performance.

The divergence between Copilot for Microsoft 365 and the knowledge management tools in the IDC surveys might be the difference between general and company-specific applications. Addressing the specific needs of an employee, so they feel like they are seen as an individual with unique qualities and needs, is the goal.

Opposite: AI-powered knowledge management tools can "coach" customer support representatives.

Tarot Reader

The clerk, colleague, and coach are useful, calculative personas; but pushing beyond their limitations can open other views and contexts. One potential territory is the tarot.

Tarot is a set of 78 cards used for self-reflection or guidance that originated in fifteenth-century Europe. One proposes a question, shuffles the deck, draws the cards, and places them in a predetermined pattern. Then the meaning of each card is interpreted based on their position and the overall context of the question.

Carl Jung believed that the tarot is a visible manifestation of the connection between the conscious and unconscious mind, and that we have an "internal tarot" made up the fundamental images that form the collective consciousness, or archetypes. Although they have an esoteric association, tarot cards are not necessarily mystical, nor do they foretell the future. They are a different kind of tool, similar to Eno's Oblique Strategies, to help shift one's perception.

Because LLMs draw from the collective conscious (the Internet), there is a beguiling parallel through the tarot to Jung's concept of the collective unconscious. So the potential exists to use generative AI output, not as answers, but as provocations. This requires a different kind of prompt, intended to add friction and generate something which does not conform to expected outcomes.

In a 2024 conversation with actor Stephen Fry, Eno wondered aloud how one might alter their prompts in such a way that they are forced to do something interesting. They would have to be prepared to close off what he called "all the avenues of mediocrity." It then would be an exercise in trying to force the system to do something that is against its nature, which is to generate the next probable thing. We would want the improbable thing.

This would be material thinking instead of representational thinking. It would be working through the problem in a lateral, active way. The results could be used as is: include it in the deck, make it the illustration, let it be the headline. Or the results could become like a tarot card: as something to be interpreted, a key to another truth, a guide in new territory. In any case, if AI can handle the boring and repetitive, then what remains includes space for the chaotic, inexplicable humanity that is still our domain.

Opposite: Generative AI output can be used as a modern "tarot" for tapping into one's unconscious mind; offering guidance and reflection.

Altering the Customer Journey

We have established how technology reframes the world. Within the world of branding, the customer journey functions as a fundamental framing tool. It tracks the transformation of a person from potential customer to user, and hopefully on to advocacy. Focusing on the customer's experience determines brand touchpoints, or points of interaction from logo to transaction to customer service. While it adapts to the specificities of each brand, the customer journey generally serves as a checklist against a brand's offerings. Then ideally, any friction or problem is resolved, and future actions are planned out.

Traditionally, the customer journey begins with awareness, then moves on to information gathering. An advertisement is seen by someone whose curiosity then leads them to learn more about the brand. But what happens when advertising and search, as we currently know it, disappears?

Beginning in 2023, Google began to roll out search results which, instead of placing paid or algorithmically-weighed results at the top, offered AI-generated text responses that were conversational in tone. This is one of many initial steps toward what is known as agentic AI, the emergence of AI agents acting with a degree of autonomy. Individuals set up a personal agent that is then empowered to act on their behalf. One could look to the 2013 Spike Jonze film *Her* for a lovely example of an AI agent that psychologically adapts to the user Theodore's individuality, and later, without asking, submits his work to a publisher.

Having a clerk/colleague/coach whispering into your ear and helping you achieve your goals is a captivating idea. Granted, it will take years of development before any agent reaches the benchmarks set in *Her*, but the thought experiment seems to solidify the potential for an I-Thou subjective relationship.

Recent work is already showing promise. A November 2024 paper, "Generative Agent Simulations of 1,000 People," written by a team including researchers from Stanford and Google DeepMind, describes the process where 1,000 recruits were interviewed by an AI model, followed by surveys and experiments. The interviews combined scripted and adaptive follow-up questions that were open-ended to gain idiographic knowledge about each individual. Then based on their responses, a generative agent was created for each individual. To evaluate the agents, both they and the human participants completed the same surveys and experiments. The accuracy of the agents was evaluated by comparing their responses to the original human responses, taking into consideration the consistency of both rounds done by the human participants. Given the concerns about AI's algorithmic bias toward underrepresented populations, researchers performed subgroup analyses of dimensions including political ideology, race, and gender.

The results were promising, with an 85 percent similarity in responses between the human participants and the AI-generated agents, and with ideological and race discrepancies loosely dropping by half. Gender-based discrepancy remained approximately the same, with the research team attributing that to the disparity's already low level.

As synthetic personas remain in the early stages of development, a host of potential applications presents itself. It is human nature to prefer one teacher over another, one restaurant server over another, or one government bureaucrat over another. We just harmonize differently with different people.

So the ability to select a search result persona is a small step beyond the ability to select a voice in current generations of digital assistants. Only now, instead of being limited to language, gender, and accents, we can tune in affability, degrees of sarcasm, or proclivities for dad jokes. And in order for the persona to establish an emotional connection, it most likely will be programed in a manner like the Stanford/Google DeepMind team.

Opposite: Current methods can generate personal digital agents whose responses match their human subjects with an 85 percent similarity.

MIDJOURNEY://A BLACK AND WHITE IMAGE ON 35 MM FILM OF A YOUNG MAN STANDING NEXT TO HIS SOUL.

Now search, at least in the case of Google's original incarnation, was based on reliability as determined by linkage. The original programming weighed sites that had links going out, as well as coming in, more than standalone sites. Persona-enhanced search would do that, with a pinch of what could be called an opinion, bringing the search experience closer to curation or, better yet, listening to a really good disc jockey. In other words, taste.

It is easy to tell when a persona has taste or not. Tools like Google's NotebookLM are designed to help users interact with various documents. It can summarize or answer specific questions about the material, and it can even generate an audio overview that sounds like a podcast conversation between two jovial people. This is fine when a user is pressed for time, but if one intends to derive anything meaningful from listening, they quickly realize that the conversation is drivel: regurgitated material, without any critical insight.

For example, if one searches for information on Bob Dylan, a predictive AI algorithm will generate results populated with tangentially-related news items, or pull from widely-distributed press material. But if the search results were able to channel the personality of cultural critic Greil Marcus—a revered figure whose work situates rock music in the American cultural and political landscape—the results would have a totally different contour and carry more gravitas.

Luckily, technology eventually becomes more affordable, and the asymmetry of tools balances out. Equally inevitable are individual users overlaying their AI-generated personas onto their own digital agents, and sending them out into the world to do their bidding.

We now have a situation where an individual's exposure to brands is mediated by a digital agent. And brands will most likely use their own agents as influencers or emissaries. So instead of the previous model of a direct brand-customer relationship, there is a brand-agent-agent-customer chain. If brands are emotional associations held in the mind, how is that connection initiated in such an extra-mediated relationship?

Because search is fundamentally changed, the existing advertising landscape—with its programmatic ad placement, sponsorships, and advertorials—now has an extra gatekeeper to contend with, in the form of an extra-vigilant digital agent. And when that agent is sent to find and purchase a pristine pair of white leather sneakers with

Opposite: Mediating brand interaction through digital agents is like a puppet speaking to another puppet.

MIDJOURNEY:// TWO HANDS WITH SOCK PUPPETS.

light-reflective panels on the side, the way in which it was trained introduces unforeseen parameters. For example: if the user feels strongly about the way AI hoovers up all the content on the web, they may impose that ethical position and prevent the agent from working around any paywalls. Then any press that the sneaker company may have received that sits behind those paywalls becomes off limits, and a potential sale is lost.

Such ethical parameters are the product of logic and emotion. And the question about shopping agents is how they behave in categories where purchases are more emotional than rational. The Stanford/Google DeepMind persona work is promising, as is the incredible ability for LLMs to find connective, almost synesthetic, relationships between disparate categories: jazz is blue, the smell of incense is round, or warm milk tastes sleepy. So it is within reason to ask your shopping agent to find a bag that is more lumberjack than office worker. The results will probably come pretty close to how you want that bag to look and feel, thus turning your AI agent into a strange combination of clerk, colleague, and shopping tarot reader.

Designer and AI engineer Ali Madad presents the AI personas that he builds for clients as "equipped with simulated customer profiles and behaviors, capable of responding to real-time events, evolving through interactions, and performing tasks such as content creation, moderation, and engagement. They can buy and sell things—have their own virtual credit cards, etc."

The question on the other side of the equation is the "motivation" of brand agents, and whose side they are really on. Yes, the potential for exploitative or even nefarious action exists, but as the growing skepticism about the effects of social media on mental and political health indicates, those ill intents always come under scrutiny.

Any brand that leans more toward corporate exploitation than the richer potential of individualized subjective relationships probably won't be around that long. Knowing that a brand is partnering with me to fulfill my life's objectives deepens my trust. Right now, with the current state of AI, that demonstration of care tends to be performative. But once we achieve a deeper lever of individualization, much of the friction and distrust in brand relationships dissipates.

Because if there isn't a pro-Starbucks that isn't pro-me, then it isn't pro-Starbucks.[1]

Opposite: Ali Madad's categories of AI personas.

New McKinsey

Management consulting, like McKinsey & Company, emphasizing the potential to help companies cut costs and optimize efficiency.

New Species

A new kind of intelligence, potentially as different from humans as humans are from other species, emphasizing the uniqueness and unpredictability of AI's development and capabilities.

Shoggoth (Lovecraft)

An undefined entity that can take on various interpretations, underlining the elusive and multifaceted nature of AI.

Stochastic Parrots

Systems that haphazardly stitch together sequences from their vast training data, focusing more on probabilistic combinations rather than meaningful understanding.

Paperclip Maximizer

This thought experiment presents AI as potentially focusing on a narrow goal to the exclusion of all else, illustrating the dangers of misaligned objectives.

Smart Intern

A diligent intern requiring supervision and direction, rapidly assimilating vast information, piecing it together but missing true comprehension.

Personal Copilot

Skillfully assists with data navigation, and can supplement and augment its operator's aim and intent.

Blurry JPEG of the Web

A pixelated, imprecise representation, capturing the essence but missing the finer, clearer details.

Puppy Love

Maybe the closest metaphor for the ideal personal agent would be a dog. The general theme of evolution centers on the survival of the fittest, with the dog's evolutionary success better described as the survival of the friendliest. Dogs extend constant attention to the actions and emotional state of the people around them, performing a pretty good approximation of an I-Thou, subjective relationship. They are constantly on alert for anything out of the ordinary—a stranger at the door, an odd sound in the basement—and they constantly monitor and respond to even our slightest movements. We can be cutting food for the family, and if we just angle the knife just so ... your dog instantly knows the next piece is for them—before you even finish cutting.

That link between our inner lives and our physicality is almost instantaneous and often unconscious. Probably the best indicator of an idea's physical affect are goosebumps. They are immediate, uncontrollable, and ultimately cannot be hidden. Therefore, biometric tracking—in the training of agents, as an indicator in market analysis, or as a source for product improvement—is rich for exploration. Biometric tracking's history goes back at least as far as 1879 when French ophthalmologist Louis Émile Javal noticed how readers' eyes scan across text with quick movements (what he called "saccades") punctuated with short pauses ("visual fixations"). The first (overly intrusive) eye tracking device arrived in 1908, and over approximately eight decades of refinement, it was used to observe how people consumed content, specifically product and service offerings. Since then eye tracking has been used to learn what audiences see and ignore, offering valuable insight into behaviors and intentions.

Putting de Bono's "Black Hat" aside, we do need to acknowledge that our current state of "surveillance capitalism" which has instrumentalized "human behaviour for the purposes of modification and monetization"[2] needs some sort of reframing. This technological determinist mindset has yet to fully conform to society's needs, requirements, and desires. And there is nothing to say that biometric tracking is only useful in oppressive police states. The metaphorical horses of facial recognition and biometric tracking have already left the barn, and these databases are widely shared and currently available in countries you have yet to visit. The security systems in many international airports already check your documents against your face, and getting to your flight is much faster because of that.

Opposite: Eye tracking can offer valuable insight into audience behaviors and intentions.

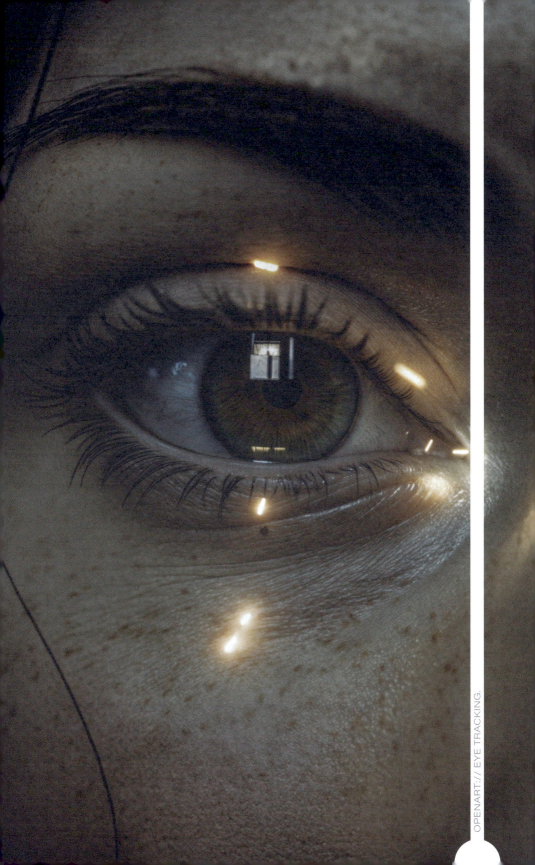

At the 2024 Cambridge Festival, historian Dr. Jonnie Penn proposed looking at the printing press for an analogy. It took 400 years to access the benefits of printing, mainly mass literacy. But that didn't happen until society instituted free education and the cost of paper went down. Then asking what is the better invention—the Internet or the weekend—he pointed out that society formalizes the routines and procedures we agree to live within.

This is where a bit of meditative thinking, along with a brander's attention to material effect, and emotional affect, can be helpful. The branding profession can lead through example by emphasizing greater equity through the measured combination of biometrics and AI's predictive powers. For example, Clear Secure calls itself "an identity company that powers effortless experiences wherever you go." Beginning in 2003, Clear, as it is publicly known, set up rapid pre-check stations at a handful of airport security lines across the United States. Originally based on facial, iris, and fingerprint scans, it introduced high-resolution, wide-angle cameras to identify users in 2024. And in personal conversation, employees have shared the vision where a member could leave their wallet at home and still take a cab to the airport, board the plane, and pay for their meals and hotel at their destination, all through Clear verification.

As Clear is expanding across North America and Western Europe, and partnering with hospitals, concert venues, and sports arenas—expediting security control and verifying identity—it is also seen as elitist. And there are people in the world who refuse to pay for membership because it only reinforces financial classification. Now imagine the company adding a person's gait to their verification criteria and offering airport security access for free—only taking license fees from each airport and venue that offers it—and transforming into a payment platform. If widely adapted, the money generated by small transaction fees would outweigh the airport line memberships. And then airport security lines would be more like the electronic toll systems used on roads, bridges, and tunnels around the world: frictionless.

While there are initial forays in AI and biometric legislation across the globe, whole sections of leadership still need exactly these kinds of thought experiments, object lessons, and social pressure when formulating policy. It is permissible and necessary to cultivate excitement by the possibilities for the equitable distribution of knowledge and learning, and about the potential for human development and flourishing.

Opposite: What is the better invention: the Internet or the weekend?

RECRAFT:// OFFICE WORKER WORKING ON THEIR LAPTOP COMPUTER WHILE SITTING ON A BEACH. A TROPICAL DRINK IS ON A TABLE NEXT TO THEM.

Keeping It Together

So extrapolating from there, as search undergoes transformation, so does security and systems regulation. It is not too far-fetched to foresee the moment when the rhythm of one's fingers on the keyboard, the accelerometers in one's phone, or the heart rate monitors in one's watch unite into a more accurate verification of identity than a forgettable password. Your devices know you as well as your dog. And like a dog, they attend to your every move, as well as anticipate what you are about to do.

Amazon's Subscribe & Save, introduced in 2007, allows customers to set up scheduled deliveries for regularly consumed items such as breakfast cereal, toothpaste, or pet food. And it could be argued that knowing that one no longer needed to check inventory on such mundane items, freed up a good deal of mental space and helped avoid trips to the store or online checkouts. Convenience is an easy sell. And Amazon's preexisting partnerships with vendors, combined with volume-based savings and market share, make a compelling case for customers to subscribe to toilet paper—as ridiculous as that may sound.

But if your digital agent has access to your schedule, travel plans, upcoming nights out with friends, work events, streaming content tendencies, the weather, your outdoor exercise routine, comments on your social media feeds, the inventory of your pantry, and a whole host of data—from the significant to the easily overlooked—the potential for it to regulate the basics of your life becomes irresistible. A well-trained and integrated digital assistant can take care of the maintenance of you, and render all the subscription-monitoring or double-payment monitoring apps, all the personal finance apps, all the package tracking apps irrelevant.

In effect, a properly-calibrated digital agent reduces the noise of everyday decisions and is capable of making optimal decisions better than humans. The idea of bounded rationality, from the American psychologist Herbert A. Simon, defines the limitations of choice. People may want to make the best decision, but often accept the satisfactory over the optimal because an optimal decision requires adequate time, information, willpower, and cognitive capacity—quantities that are not always available to people going about their everyday life.

After Simon's foundational work, the psychologists Amos Tversky and Daniel Kahneman proposed their prospect theory, which states that people make choices based on perceptions of losses or gains, as measured against an individually-perceived reference point, and that they feel losses asymmetrically greater than an equivalent gain.

So handing off actions such as paying bills, keeping an eye out for seasonal sales, or restocking pantry items changes the dynamics of the exchange on the most transactional level. And allowing a digital agent to complete a more significant task such as booking airline tickets mitigates decision anxiety on a more emotional level. A great number of moments and touchpoints along the customer journey will be transformed and revalued as the power-dynamics of decision-making shift.

Brand OS

Because digital agents also act on behalf of brands, the customer journey is altered. Traditionally, brands would begin with a consistent metaphorical approach in their messaging. Coca-Cola, for example, insisted on a proper mix of "intrinsics" and "extrinsics" in all communications and packaging. Intrinsics would be representations of the product's flavor, the carbonated bubbles, the chill of the ideal serving

---

Opposite: A well-trained and integrated digital assistant can assist in choosing between similar items.

temperature; extrinsics would be the effect after drinking the product: smiles, family gatherings, and rainbows. Any alterations or new product introductions would be in response to customer response or market trends, such as OK Soda, which was their contribution to the ironic disillusionment running through music and television of the mid-1990s. While the vibe of being just "OK" may have been spot on, the extrinsic marketing was more captivating than the product's intrinsics.

Agencies like Ogilvy contributed to the toolbox of metaphors with their Brand OS. Pictured as a layered sphere similar to the Earth, the core represents a brand's authenticity that persists through all events. The mantle represents competitive shifts and responses to external events, which still need to answer back to the values at the core. And the crust, depicted as a pixelated geodesic dome, represents immediate and reactive behavior within fast moving events. While relatively simple, Ogilvy's Brand OS is a perfectly workable decision-making tool. But it, along with all the other approaches found in agencies and branding departments in the profession, is still subject to the bounded rationality of the people at the helm, as measured against the traditional customer journey map.

Ali Madad proposes a Brand OS, which is an AI agent tasked with market analysis, threat assessment, predictive modeling, scheduling, supply chain logistics ... basically anything imaginable and actionable. Madad's Brand OS can take any publicly-available metric—social media comments, news reports, competitive product launches, currency fluctuations—and then compile that information to propose designs, find ideal vendors, or suggest more efficient delivery routes. Such a system would capture previously-overlooked touchpoints along the customer journey, and identify new touchpoints, casting a wider and faster net, reinventing what used to be called "desk research," and surpassing the current correlative limits of big data. Actions still need to be approved by humans, but they would now be armed with a more rational loss/gain assessment.

Agents Gone Wild

The magic of capitalism is its ability to monetize anything. Brand valuation combines share price with a tally of every impression of a brand asset from logo, to tag line, to product placement in a film. Social media companies monetize heightened emotions. The search engine optimization industry auctions off words to advertisers, in real time, as they are typed into Google. People are paid to observe and participate in consumer focus groups.

The reliability of focus groups is suspect. When asked to respond to a proposed product or service, responses arrive on two levels, what Kahneman called System 1 and System 2. System 1 is unconscious, fast, and intuitive. It's the immediate "ick" or "ooooh" at first glance, and is based on patterns and experiences. System 2 is slow, methodical, and requires analytical effort. System 1 is error prone, while System 2 is more reliable. System 1 is impulsive, System 2 offers self-control.

As a way to qualm executive anxiety or rationalize decisions, focus groups are socially important. As reliable qualitative surveys, focus groups are affected by group dynamics and irrelevant interactions. Not everyone is as open in front of other people as someone else might be.

Above: Future consumer focus groups can foreseeably be comprised of AI personas.

Opposite: Ali Madad proposes a Brand OS/AI agent which could surpass the current limits of big data, offering more-rational suggestions and inputs for human operators.

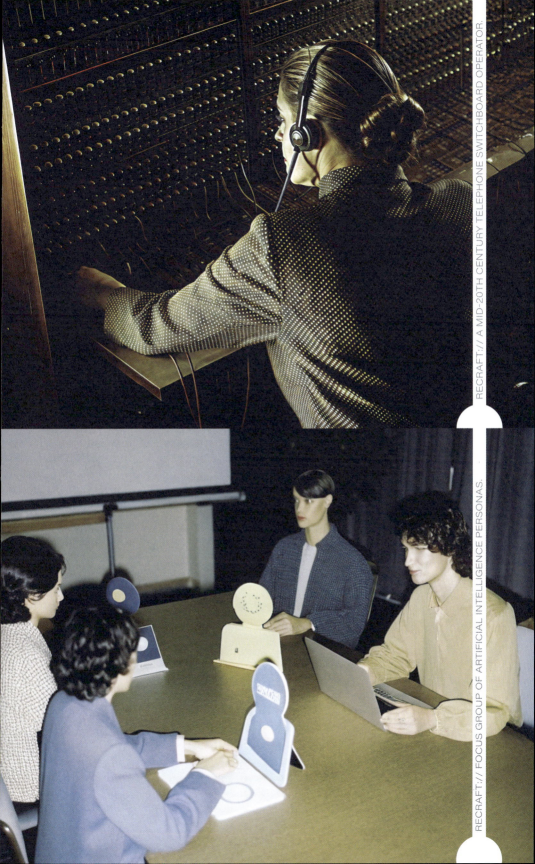

Or they might dominate the conversation and exert undue influence on other participants. The best outcome of a focus group would be an immediate System 1 response to a pink cupcake versus a blue one. A considered, thought-out opinion on wealth management products, probably not so much. That is the sort of product better suited for a survey where a participant ranks responses to a series of questions on a scale of very doubtful to most definitely. Unfortunately, those surveys tend to be overly leading and do not allow for discursive System 2 analysis.

This is where the Generative Agent Simulations work from Stanford and Google DeepMind becomes valuable in a collaborative marketplace similar to Amazon's Mechanical Turk. Virtual focus groups could be run with teams of personalized agents. If the agent personas reflect the original human personas with the kind of accuracy suggested in the initially-published paper, then there is no longer any need to fly to Kansas City to sit in a mirrored room and evaluate a new lipstick. Most researchers suggest running several focus groups of like-minded people to get the best results. With simulated personas, more groups, composed of even more like-minded points of view can be run quicker and cheaper, with responses free of interpersonal influence.

Personalized agents would become even more valuable to marketers and brands if individuals allowed access to their biometric data: how they interact with their devices, finger speed, and hesitation, or whether they pinch in on a photo. MapQuest, the first free online mapping service launched in 1996 and was purchased by America Online (AOL) three years later. When Verizon bought AOL, MapQuest was part of the deal. Verizon then had the ability to correlate their customers location, via cell tower triangulation, against all the businesses on MapQuest. This rich data was valuable to advertisers, and Verizon could, in effect, double dip by selling bandwidth to customers and customer data to advertisers. Now, the more specific biometric data, combined with the persona of an individualized agent, becomes even more valuable.

We know who would purchase that data, so who would be paid? The argument could be made that renting out one's personalized agent is equivalent to offering one's time to participate in a focus group or quantitative survey. And presumably the data from a simulated persona would be more reliable than a messy, contradicting human being. Even more so if biometric data was included. It could also be an interesting way to answer the concerns sparking surveillance and data privacy legislation around the world.

Opposite: Personalized agents would become even more valuable to marketers and brands if individuals allowed access to their biometric data.

RECRAFT:// RENTING OUT YOUR DATA.

Measuring the Flow of Consciousness

The conventional thinking around people's brand decisions is based on assumptions aligned with classical economic theories. It suggests that people know what they want, have the ability to predict their own behavior, and can make logical decisions based on rational preferences. Unfortunately, this is not a solid foundation for making behavioral predictions. People are not computers. The neural networks in AI systems were based on human neurons, and not the other way around.

Beyond the emergence of AI, with the current complexities of the world, the signal to noise ratio of today's landscape is out of balance to the point where brands and marketers find themselves using old tools for new problems. Audiences are fragmented, the siloed nature of global conglomerates lead to missed insights and opportunities, and current marketing efforts often have unpredictable outcomes—such as the vehement backlash against Bud Light after they hired Dylan Mulvaney, a social media influencer who is also a transgender woman.

Opportunities are arriving where interdisciplinary groups—operating outside existing silos—can develop new analytical and connected tools that offer improved consumer strategies. The common phrase "data to wisdom" begins to capture this movement, but perhaps AI can help increase our understanding of human consciousness itself.

Basing insights on stable objects, like demographic segmentations, or binary yes/no survey responses, does not convey the complete picture because consumer insights are not just about the consumer at a moment in time. They are about the consumer acting within an ecosystem that is much larger than the brand, which means brands have to track movement between customers, the business, and the world at large.

The philosopher Gilles Deleuze claimed that a general theory of society must be a generalized theory of flows. Though this is an elliptical concept, he described how something as simple and static as color can capture movement in a lecture at Vincennes/Saint-Denis:

"Color" can be said to have a dark side, since it is the darkening of light. No doubt it's also the illumination of black. It is the darkening of white as well as the illumination of black—and how does it darken white? ... Due to the dark aspect of color, darkened light, color is inseparable from movement. —Gilles Deleuze[3]

Opposite: Perhaps AI can help increase our understanding of human consciousness.

Deleuze's flow is in line with one of the oldest concepts in western thought: that all objects are in the process of becoming something else. Rocks become sand, seeds become trees, children become adults. Flow also works with contemporary economic theory, notably in John Maynard Keynes' theory of the circular flow of money: one person's spending goes toward another's earnings, and when that person spends her earnings, she is supporting another's spending. Wealth is not the momentary measure of how much capital one has, but the amount of capital passing through one's account.

Customer insights operate in an economy of attention and behaviors. And AI can help measure the flow of attention and intention by measuring states of change, and vectors rather than positions.

We only know the world through our relationship with it. And if we see consciousness as our lived experience of a confluence of forces, then closely tracing the "recruitment strategy" of individual gestures through biometrics—along with location, history, and any number of predictive connections generated by AI—may just get us close to actually measuring consciousness.

Close, not perfect. Because that pesky Heisenberg Uncertainty Problem says it is impossible to simultaneously know both the position and momentum of an object with perfect accuracy. Measuring one offsets the other. Still, these new tools can offer a much more nuanced understanding of the relationship between people and brands than the customer journey. And such a nuanced understanding brings brands and people closer to an I-Thou relationship that considers, and potentially enhances, the subjective needs of each individual.

1   From a conversation with Tom Guarriello, Ph.D.

2   Norma Möllers, David Murakami Wood, & David Lyon, "Surveillance Capitalism: An Interview with Shoshana Zuboff," in *Surveillance and Society*, 17 (2019), Surveillance Studies Centre, Queen's University, Canada.

3   Gilles Deleuze, "Painting and the Question of Concepts," lecture series, number 6 (May 19, 1981).

Opposite: Wealth is not the momentary measure of how much capital one has, but the amount of capital passing through one's account.

RECRAFT:// WEALTH IS THE AMOUNT OF ENERGY PASSING THROUGH ONE'S LIFE.

Look, Feel, Tone

If AI profoundly shifts the customer journey—how it is perceived by customers, and how it is used by brands—then obviously it affects both the creation and phenomenological weight of touchpoints along that journey.

Phenomenology is a division of philosophy and sociological research that sees all meaning and value as products of human lived experience. We perceive "presentations"—a term introduced by the early phenomenologist Franz Brentano, and a stand-in here for "touchpoint"—which are then "presented" through our sensory apparatus to our consciousness. So like the brand-agent-agent-customer chain, our personal experience is a presentation-presentation of presentation-consciousness-association chain. Now what makes that relevant for our purposes is that associations are influenced by past experience. We compare each phenomena against other experiences and the associated meanings that we have developed, then ascribe meaning.

When we experience a phenomena similar to a previous experience, the potential to build a distinctly-different meaning or association is influenced, or in the case of cognitive fatigue, it barely registers. This condition is particularly pervasive today due to the combination of algorithmic flattening and social media, and nicely-described by technology writer Kyle Chayka.

Whether visual art, music, film, literature, or choreography, algorithmic recommendations and the feeds that they populate mediate our relationship to culture, guiding our attention toward the things that fit best within the structures of digital platforms ... Algorithmic recommendations dictate genres of culture by rewarding particular tropes with promotion in feeds, based on what immediately attracts the most attention. —Kyle Chayka[1]

If you ever wondered why everything around you looks the same, and why you see the same retail chains in cities across the world, a lot of the reason stems from the algorithmic push toward the middle. The distribution of audience appreciation is heaviest toward the middle, and algorithms reward the objects that fall there with increased visibility. Which, in turn, normalizes aesthetic conformity and reinforces audience taste for more of the same.

This is further compounded in generative platforms. Since the interface is a dialog box, all the operator has to do is describe a fitting result. And because the finish is just *so perfect*, and the result was realized with predictive algorithms, the tendency to accept the outcome as presented is tempting. And why not? A well-written prompt is not that different from a creative brief. It's just in a different form.

While there will be a hundred suggestions for the best sequence and components of a prompt, they are basically variations on general themes. For example, one begins by describing the desired output and the goal, then format instructions, any pertinent warnings or parameters, and any contextual information that would help improve the final results. The process is frictionless and smooth. No bumps along the way. And potentially, no trace of the hand or the individual voice. It is the product of representational thinking: platonic and centered on the ideal.

French philosopher Roland Barthes wrote an essay, "The Third Meaning," which analyzes the orders of meaning in images. The first order, at the surface, is the informative. The basic information of who, what, where, and how. In brand usage, it is the web address, the instructions for use, the name of the brand, and other basic business. The second order is the symbolic or connotative meaning: the feeling or associations beyond literal definitions. An example would be describing an American-made truck as patriotic or proud. The truck itself is incapable of patriotism or pride, but within its surrounding

Opposite: Coffee shops tend to look alike because algorithms normalize aesthetic conformity, reinforcing the audience's taste for more of the same.

context, it can convey those attributes. Here, symbolic meaning is intentional, obvious, and draws from the common lexicon.

The third meaning falls outside of description because it is obtuse and wholly an individualized experience within an individual's consciousness.

> *This accent ... does not tend in the direction of meaning as in hysteria. It does not theatricalize ... it does not even indicate an elsewhere of meaning (another content, added to the obvious meaning); it rather frustrates meaning—subverting not the content but the entire practice of meaning. Obtuse meaning, a new practice—rare and asserted against a prevailing one, that of the signification—inevitably appears as a luxury, an expenditure without exchange; this luxury does not yet belong to today's politics, although it is already part of tomorrow's.*
> —Roland Barthes[2]

In his *Camera Lucida*, Barthes dances between the second and third order of meaning by introducing the concept of the "punctum." He poetically describes it as "A photograph's punctum is that accident which pricks me (but also bruises me, is poignant to me)." The punctum dances between the second and third orders of meaning. The symbolic has potential to touch the heart as much as the obtuse. In both cases, the affect is highly personal and subjective.

This is not to say that generative AI is incapable of having a subjective affect. Actually, quite the opposite. But it does question arguments made by people in the creative industries.

Creatives

As a term, using the word "creative" to describe a class of people—instead of the much more descriptive *illustrator, photographer, designer,* or *writer*—may be easy and intended to be complimentary, but it also has a categorical minimizing effect where the pride of craft is stripped away, leaving the just the task. But, generative AI will certainly open new territory for a different flavor of creative. So for the sake of the contingent, "creative" is currently the best tool at hand.

The main argument that the current cohort of creatives have with generative AI is how large language models (LLMs) draw from everything

Opposite: The punctum touches the heart with a highly personal and subjective affect.

on the Internet—even if it is behind a paywall—and use that corpus as source material and predictive model without proper attribution or compensation. This is not a secret. In fact, if one goes into a generative platform such as Midjourney and asks it to write a prompt for an image, the response will often include something along the lines of "in the style of _____." Given the amount of time and effort one puts into developing their own methods and approach, turning that into a style cue feels marginalizing and reductive.

For a counterargument, all one needs to do is look at how creative people are trained or developed. One does not come into the world knowing that they want to be say, a photographer. At some point in their life, they see a photograph that connects in some way, becoming a model for how they would like to live from that moment onward. Then, it is a matter of looking at all photographs, developing a criteria for evaluating images, building a personal approach to making pictures, then applying all that into a body of work.

At the beginning of photography, the other visual arts did not fully welcome it as an art form mainly because the physical body was not as evident as a brush stroke or the variation of a drawn line. But eventually, and after enough work was produced, the "eye"—the way of seeing, the sensibility of framing, the choice of subject, how the images were presented—could be discerned. And photography rose to the level of art. Yes, the technology came together where all one needed to do was press a shutter, but it still needed the individual photographer, a subject, a moment in time, media, and light to gather into a finished image.

Value in art comes from its ability to propagate the form. As more photographers of note arrived, standout individuals would push the form in some way to open more territory, rewrite definitions, and establish new traditions that further solidified photography's role. And with that firm presence, comes accepted tastes and behaviors. There is a way to be a photographer, a way of talking about photography, and a way of consuming photography that acts as a common language for anyone with a shared interest. All of that comes with some degree of pain, whether it be continued self-doubt or time spent on the outside of convention, waiting for recognition and acceptance.

And that investment in time, materials, effort, and emotional commitment is hard to leave behind when something else arrives to threaten that status quo. They cannot be recovered, so the tendency to continue—known as sunk cost fallacy—persists.

Opposite: All artist's work, regardless of their chosen media, contains aspects of other artworks.

RECRAFT:// AN ARTIST'S WORK CONTAINS ASPECTS OF OTHER ARTWORKS.

This is especially true in higher education where generational conflicts play out daily. Instructors came of age with Adobe's Photoshop, Illustrator, and InDesign, all of which were the gold standard for high-quality production. But Adobe software has never been inexpensive, especially for nonprofessionals. So students use free or lower cost platforms such as Canva or Procreate, which are not able to produce the level of high-resolution files acceptable in a professional environment, but still are able to produce work good enough for class.

The overlooked irony is that before Adobe, professional creatives relied on typesetters, photo retouchers, comp houses, dye-transfer artists, and all sorts of craftspeople in the conception and production of brands. And before generative AI platforms, creatives looked to other creatives for inspiration and influence. Nobody can say that their work does not contain aspects of other artist's work. *Nihil sub sole novum*: there is nothing new under the sun.

The introduction of digital software opened greater levels of expression and unlocked the inner mind's eye. Typography before the computer reflected the order of the typesetting machine, with anything more expressive requiring that it either be drawn or assembled by hand. After the computer, type could be stretched, squished, stacked, twisted, and altered with incredible ease. Photography before the computer reflected the materials and processes of film manufacture, camera equipment, chemistry, and photo retouchers. After the computer, the moon in a landscape could be repositioned and recolored in a matter of seconds. This fluidity and speed occurred across all creative domains: from the ability of Auto-Tune to bring individual notes into perfect pitch, to removing the necessary amount of specification time required to construct the components of a cloud-like Frank Gehry building. Every new capability, every degree of efficiency, every second saved, every new culture worker able to easily access a domain was a validation of ideas offered by Babbage and Taylor.

Digital software was also a step in the gradual commodification of design. As software made quick turnaround times possible, the expectations of the chain of production increased. The disconnect between client support and creative departments continued, if not worsened. Where once a graphic design change required sending out for new typography, waiting for it to arrive the next morning, taping a mechanical board down, heating up hot wax, putting the revisions in place, checking to see if it was square, and re-specifying the printing instruction overlay, now all a creative needed to do was just hit a button on the computer.

That removal of hand skills lowered the barriers to entry so anyone with Wi-Fi access and the right software could believably call themselves a designer. The accessibility to design history and current trends opened up with the introduction of the World Wide Web, and then social media. Libraries, classrooms, and professional organizations, once the bastions of taste and knowledge, were rendered unnecessary because all that information and connectivity was available online, immediately. The borders between what was considered good or bad, professional or amateur, accessible or obscure were redrawn or even erased. Notoriety, once the product of sustained effort and a bit of luck, was now, with the right social media post, instantaneous and ephemeral, because something better was certainly going to appear further along the feed.

The parameters of time for notoriety has shifted from the mythological to the historic to the atomized. The mythological is reserved for early masters like Paul Rand, Edward Weston, J. C. Leyendecker, Ludwig Mies van der Rohe; men—usually men—whose work established professional attitudes and approaches. The historical covers significant figures of the decade or two before the Internet's decimation of traditional media: Tibor Kalman, Guy Bourdin, Antonio Lopez, James Wines; again, usually men who set the tone for much of the work today. Younger generations may not know the names, but they are very familiar with the tone.

Atomized time is the constant now, the reductio ad absurdum of *quart d'heure de célébrité*[3] (fifteen minutes of fame), an idea from novelist Alphonse Daudet that is often misattributed to Andy Warhol. And it is a perfect accompaniment to design's overall waning of affect. There is so much good design—really, really good design—available everywhere. Social media is a constant stream of appealing, beautifully-designed objects and environments, all within the capability and reach of designers and consumers everywhere. In fact, one could argue that there is almost too much good design. Nothing succeeds like excess.

And nothing is more American than excess. After the Second World War, New York's Museum of Modern Art (MoMA) shaped international consumer culture through their ambitious Good Design program. The traveling exhibition *Design for Use, USA* (1950-52) toured Europe under the sponsorship of the State Department. Its curator, Edgar Kaufmann, Jr., architect, professor, and son of the Kaufmann's department store founder, selected items for the exhibit with a criteria of "eye appeal, function, construction and price."[4]

This basically is the average agency creative brief, as well as an apt framework for design appearing on social media: attractive, well made, affordable, and serving a purpose. To possess or be seen with good design on one's social media feed solidifies one's place in the world. This is where the feed echoes an idea from French theorist Guy Debord. To Debord, mass media had transformed modern life into a spectacle that was "not a collection of images, but a social relation among people, mediated by images."[5] This is not so foreign an idea to us. We signal vacation with an image of a beach framed by our feet, and instead of giving thanks before a wonderful meal, we have an impromptu photoshoot.

Kaufmann's exhibition and Debord's spectacle both operate on the level of the symbolic, and order life through representational thinking. "That which appears is good, that which is good appears."[6] The bad can appear only if wrapped in the good—as a fundraiser, or as virtue signaling—positive representations of positive thoughts.

In the 1980s, Tibor Kalman had a column in the *Journal of the American Institute of Graphic Arts* (AIGA) where he answered questions and generally opined about the state of graphic design. A devoted lover of what was called "vernacular design"—the work of often anonymous designers operating outside what was considered high design—he once made the observation that the general output of designers was improving. And it had reached the point where the work was so good that its level of skill defined a new mediocre.

Generative AI now offers the ability for anyone to produce almost-perfect designs, regardless of their position along the vernacular design to high design spectrum. And the need to situate the work in design history, or general visual history, is removed in atomized time. This places design and designers in a strange condition.

From the beginning of the branding profession in the mid-twentieth century, a brand's visual presence has enjoyed a place of primacy. Perhaps it was a result of the resources required to produce a package, an advertisement, or a product. And perhaps the centralization of the media and retail landscape—a handful of television networks, prominent national magazines, shopping malls—boosted the efficacy of all brand touchpoints to a stronger degree than in today's fractured, multivalent, algorithmically-personalized world where everyone's feed is unique to them.

Opposite: Vernacular design is outside any academic tradition and is often done without professional guidance.

RECRAFT:// A LOG CABIN. HIGHLY PHOTOREALISTIC.

Not only has the design profession been commoditized, so has its tools. There was probably no greater indication that the uniqueness of a design career had disappeared than in 2020 when Adobe began to run television commercials for its Creative Cloud internationally. One commercial, which had the internal name of "Fantastic Voyage," began with a shot of a subway car interior. As one rider, a young woman, begins to look around the car, it, as well as her fellow riders, begin to transform. The floor becomes a grassy meadow, riders turn into animals or cartoon figures, the camera zooms out to show the train moving through the sky toward a fantastic city, a gigantic octopus envelopes the car, then she calmly gets off at her stop and makes her way through a city full of surreal figures.

> *Nothing is off limits to your imagination. "Fantastic Voyage" showcases Adobe Photoshop as more than just a tool, it's a vehicle to help you reimagine our world's canvas. It's never been more important than right now to see things in new perspectives, play with reality, and ignite your creativity.* —AJ Joseph, chief creative director, Adobe[7]

Of course, creativity is a commodity as well. And this approach shows how entrenched the design profession is at the beginning of the age of AI. The team behind "Fantastic Voyage" still thinks in symbolic images: the advertisement sticks to the traditional 30-second commercial form and the images *represent* creativity, as opposed to personifying it.

And this is where an opportunity presents itself. The greatest sin creatives commit is the sin of pride. There is an obvious sense of satisfaction in creating something with excellent "eye appeal, function, and construction." This cannot be denied to anyone working with a good heart and good intention. But the seductive nature of accomplishment can lead to solipsism and an I-mine relationship to one's work. One begins to see themself as a rigidly-defined practitioner, authentic and consistent, instead of a constantly-developing being passing through a moment in time, along with other constantly-developing beings.

If we look to our model of consciousness for an example, then one can frame their work as a recruitment strategy, where the energies of client needs, the current moment in culture, personal experience, and technology flow through the project. Informative, symbolic, legal, and aesthetic priorities still remain, but everything is reframed as a flow of subjectivity directed outward to the intended audience. Yes, in theory, this has always been the goal of creative work, but the appearance of

Opposite: An unused still from Adobe's Fantastic Voyage advertising campaign; created by Leo Natsume.

AI so profoundly shifts the definitions and relationships of what creative people do that a moment of reframing can be helpful. The expediency and quality of generative AI imagery opens real estate that then allows for creative work and branding practice to find new territory.

Theorists such as Gilles Deleuze and Félix Guattari apply the term *deterritorialization* to the process where a social structure and its context are altered, destroyed, or transformed. The components are then reconstituted into a new territory, or *reterritorialization*. Deterritorialization's effects on economies, cultures, and politics can be profoundly alienating and disorienting. One's local knowledge—of their profession, of the structures and perceived value of their work— is suddenly implicated into mega-trends where they have no recourse. Authors Alvin Toffler and Heidi Farrell used the term "futureshock" to describe the disorientation and anxiety of "too much change in too short a period of time."[8] But it is important to remember the immanent potential for even more rewarding structures and relationships brought about by deterritorialization. For instance, Automatic Teller Machines (ATMs) were first seen as a potential replacement, and threat, for bank tellers, but over time, they enhanced the teller's role to one of advisor. ATMs also reduced costs and allowed banks to open more locations.

Baby Steps

Of course as a profession, and as a society, we are just making baby steps into this new working relationship. One of the first ambitious undertakings applying generative AI to a very large, almost unmanageable project was design firm Pentagram's work for the Office of Management and Budget (OMB) and General Services Administration (GSA), both departments within the United States government. The goal was to make all the strategic goals for every government agency available to the public in an accessible, easily-understood manner. Federal law mandates that each agency's strategic planning benefit the public good. So besides being a requirement, building a one-stop portal for all this information serves the political goals of transparency and accountability. The site, Performance.gov, went live in 2011 during the Obama administration after numerous delays and months of inter-governmental beta testing. During the first Trump administration, Performance.gov announced a vision and long-term strategy

Opposite: Over time, Automatic Teller Machines (ATMs) enhanced the teller's role to one of advisor, reduced costs, and allowed more locations to open.

for a more sustainable, user-friendly site offering easier navigation in addition to an online platform for improved access to performance data to better serve stakeholders' needs.

As part of that "user-friendly" goal, Pentagram looked at how a platform like ChatGPT might summarize overly-wordy government speak, and at how they might create a coherent look and feel for a site with a potential need for thousands of icons and images—with room to grow. ChatGPT as an accepted tool used by the U.S. government, is a work in progress. Because their LLMs pull from everything on the Internet, there is a danger of classified or protected material finding its way into the public realm. So agencies interested in the platform would have to contract with ChatGPT Enterprise. Released in 2023, the service offers enterprise-grade security and privacy where prompts and company data are not used to train OpenAI models, and data encryption is present throughout. And in 2024, the United States Agency for International Development (USAID), which administers civilian foreign aid and development assistance, became the first agency to adopt ChatGPT Enterprise. This seems feasible for an agency not run by a cabinet member, and with their own rule-making authority, where something like the Department of Defense would have much more difficulty.

Much of Pentagram's effort went into illustration style and stock-photo applications. Elaborating on the initiative's logo of one red and two blue bars overlaid on a capital P, the photography proposal applied color bars over images either as focal points or just as stylistic unifiers. The illustration went a bit further by uploading simple handmade brush strokes and cut-paper shapes—geometric shapes, arrows, eyes, conversation bubbles, restricted to red, blue, and black—to Midjourney. The platform was prompted to merge everything into specified pictograms that appeared on a white background: government buildings, livestock, deserts, housing, medicine. From there, a catalog of 1,500 illustrations were generated. Resistance from the design, illustration, and segments of the AI communities was, as to be expected, vehement. Many comments stuck to the Luddite playbook of pointing out how so much work was directed away from human illustrators and designers, and how the images did not meet arbitrary standards of quality or taste. And this was just in response to a press release. Like many projects for large, fluid organizations with many layers of stakeholder buy-in, implementation has been slow and uneven. And with subsequent administrations and shifting priorities, chances are

Opposite: Pentagram's work for the United States government website Performance.gov; featuring AI-generated icons.

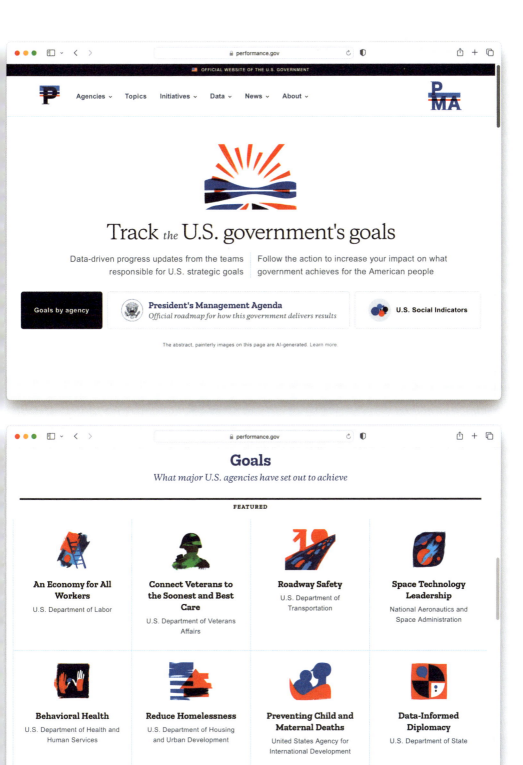

it will change. Still, it is a significant exploration into how AI might be applied to a branding program.

The program, as envisioned by Pentagram, does make very dry material more approachable. And the stylistic continuity across disparate agencies ties them together into a bigger picture that reflects the traditional United States motto of *E pluribus unum* (out of many, one). The common measure of a brand, as a verification of authenticity, still stands in the case of Performance.gov. And because the system has a friendlier tone, instead of the officious authority one would expect from government communications, there is a sense that the subjectivity of American citizens is recognized in the most inclusive manner.

Even when that sense of subjectivity is performative, an AI-enriched brand experience—the most important touchpoint—can evoke positive brand associations. Many airlines offer real-time baggage tracking through their websites or apps, and some like JetBlue, sidestep that by pushing updated information to passengers via text or email. In the scheme of all the small indignities associated with air travel, this is a relatively large win for such a small cost. A symphony of machine learning, automatic scanners, and image recognition track when each piece of luggage passes through a relevant point—boarding the plane, arriving at the destination, on its way to baggage claim—then combine that with passenger contact information, which then triggers a notification. And with upcoming improvements in image recognition, combined with machine learning algorithms, the wasteful and time consuming process of affixing paper tags and stickers will become a thing of the past. Then, all a passenger will need to do is take an image of their luggage with their smartphone and place it on the conveyor belt to baggage handling. AI-enhanced visual pre-screening of baggage can help sort, load, and optimize cargo space, which after time will lead to more efficient fuel use.

Another small, but wonderful brand moment comes in the form of machine vision systems at airport parking lots. If one is a frequent flyer, the frequent checks and permissions of the airport experience quickly becomes a death of a thousand cuts. So the relatively-recent roll-out of machine vision is a welcome step. When a traveler books a reservation at a long-term lot, they are asked for their license plate number. Then, upon arrival, all they have to do is arrive. Once the car triggers a sensor at the front gate, a small camera checks the plate

Opposite: Machine vision systems can create a seamless welcome to airport parking lots.

number against the reservation list and opens the gate—all within a few seconds. You were expected and welcome as soon as you were recognized. Just like visiting friends and family.

Seamless welcomes like this were available as early as the mid-2000s for Virgin Atlantic Upper Class customers flying out of London's Heathrow Airport. Back then, Upper Class passengers could book a car to pick them up at home, which extended the sense of care up to a person's front door. Drivers had a personal digital device that allowed them to inform the front door team when they were about to arrive. Upon arriving at the unmarked entrance, a camera confirmed the car's plate, the gate went up, and at the top of the ramp an attendant welcomed you by name and handed you your ticket.

Granted, the harsh margins of the airline industry, combined with numerous mergers, expansion of loyalty programs, and credit card rewards bonuses have made this ultra-luxurious indulgence a thing of the past. But it is rewarding to see the lessons of personalized service channeled through AI and made available to a wider section of people. And this has been the story of technology throughout human history. After the transistor was first developed in 1947, it took seven years before it was used in a practical portable radio, which went on the market priced at the 2020-equivalent of $500 U.S. dollars. And only with the appearance of integrated circuits in the early 1960 were transistorized products such as calculators and personal computers possible. Now, the transistor is the basic building block of the modern world: inexpensive and pervasive.

Language and Imperfection

Humanity's first technology has come full circle to emerge at the center of its most transformative. While platforms such as ChatGPT, Claude, Perplexity, or Pi have the ability to have an informal conversation, there still is a certain distance to the interaction. Every once in a while, an AI researcher or developer will hint at voice-based agents that speak with the same unevenness of human beings, with "umms" and "ahhhs" and false starts to sentences. The artist Marcel Duchamp called these ephemeral traces of another's presence the *inframince* (infrathin). Examples of the infrathin would be the residual body heat left behind in a chair after someone gets up, or the lingering scent of a person in an empty elevator. It is the slightest of difference between presence and absence. A whisper of just off, which can be just right.

Opposite: Duchamp's inframince (infrathin) could be the rumpled linens, imprints, and residual body heat of a recently-vacated bed.

OPENART:// VIEW FROM ABOVE. LOOKING DOWN ON AN EMPTY BED. DEPRESSIONS ON THE PILLOWS SHOW WHERE A PERSON'S HEAD WAS.

Pentagram's work on Performance.gov approaches the spirit of the infrathin. The imperfection of the illustrations is what gives them their charm. And over time, generative platforms like Midjourney seem to be acquiring the ability to perfectly create imperfect images. In the late 2000s, the creative team at Publicis proposed a campaign to Citibank which allowed for images from smartphones. At the time, any other art director would have drawn back in horror at the possibility of "amateur" images being used in a campaign for the world's largest financial services company. In the mid-2020s, the idea was spot on. Generative AI tends to produce perfect images which are centered, have a harmonious color cast, nicely composed, and all in focus. This is because generative AI platforms are programmed to give a positive result—"That which appears is good, that which is good appears." And most of the professional images on the web are exactly that. Therefore, generated images represent the photographed image, instead of the photographed world. And when generative AI attempts to capture something like feminine subjectivity, the images are modeled on images of women, instead of the lives of women. That is why they tend to be just "off."

When the model has been trained on all available language, it can be difficult to generate distinct messaging. So perhaps there is a way to inject the imperfection of life into the language and images generated by AI platforms. The off-centered, the awkwardly cropped, the thumb covering the lens, the flare of a street light, the "oops," the inhalation of breath before a long sentence … being just "off" could be just right. Writing a prompt for such mistakes approaches the dream conveyed by Stephen Fry and Brian Eno to force the system to do something that is against its nature.

Prompt writing is a form of supervised training. One might define a role, a task, and a format, or one might approach it with more detail by defining a character, issuing a request, giving examples, describing the ideal output, and then setting parameters to evaluate the results. The term given to this new class of creative is "prompt engineer," which conforms to the technical and analytical nature of the domain. But right after ChatGPT's public release, some enthusiastic commenters equated prompting to Harry Potter incantations. There is a beauty in that because it hints at the collective unconscious, both logical and illogical, running through the narratives of society. And when we measure the effect of touchpoints along the customer journey, we are in effect tracking the exchange rate between the physical and the mental, the external and the internal, the real and the dream.

Opposite: The "imperfections" of lens flares and motion blur inject a sense of real-life in images.

Trust

In a sense, our exploration of the subjective, and traces of human presence, is also a meditation on trust. How can we trust an AI agent acting on behalf of a brand? And where might that trust come from? We know that even the slightest fluctuation when interacting with something that looks alive can throw us in the uncanny valley. But when the object in question does something useful, the uncanny feeling disappears. So right away we might assume with high probability that an agent salesperson would be the wrong application of AI, while a customer service agent would be a better fit.

Generally, it is probably best not to hide whether something is an AI or not. A 2024 Lippincott Brand Aperture survey reported that 46 percent of respondents would trust a brand less if they learned that something they had assumed was human was in reality an AI. So there is a potential conflict in giving an AI a human name such as Alexa or Grace, turning up the personality, coding in a few "ummms" and verbal tics, and then letting it face the public without contextualizing it properly. If you are a technology company, and you want to show off your capabilities with some razzle dazzle, then it may be a stunt, but there is a degree of authenticity present. If you are the American Automobile Association (AAA) and you want an AI persona to handle roadside assistance calls, it is probably better to let a real human take the call but give them an AI coach to coordinate logistics.

And attention should be paid to the form in which an agent interacts with a customer. The current fallback is a chatbot, but they are impersonal, often mistakenly deployed, and tend to behave like the generic suggestion algorithms on streaming platforms. If you want to go on a vacation, the last thing you want to do is chat. Instead, you would want to see pictures of possible destinations. Hopefully the algorithm driving that display of images has insight into your preferences and avoids recommending senior citizen cruises when you are a young couple looking for a romantic getaway.

Another area in desperate need for improvement is client relationship management software (CRM). The amount of follow-up emails and texts asking if you "left something behind" when all you did was check to see if the price on a pair of sneakers had gone down, or if that set of gray linen sheets was restocked, only erodes a brand relationship. And

Opposite: Even the slightest fluctuation or strangeness when interacting with something that looks alive can throw us in the uncanny valley.

why if I just bought two pairs of jeans, am I being asked if I want to buy more jeans? In theory, CRM databases should be better integrated with inventory, buying patterns, and customer history, and then compared against specific conditions ranging anywhere from seasons, cultural trends, delivery worker strikes, or supply chain issues. A brand that is incapable of paying attention to me is a brand that sees me only as a transaction.

There is no longer any question whether AI will be as widely accepted as the computer. It is a done deal and we interact with AI assistants every day, whether we know it or not. Alexa and Siri are well-known personas, each with their own quirks and abilities. Each are front-and-center sub-brands of flagship brands: Alexa as a sub-brand of Amazon, and Siri as a sub-brand of Apple. When they work, the halo effect supports the trust given to the parent brand, and the association is strengthened.

On the other end of the spectrum, American Express uses "a machine learning-powered fraud detection model to monitor in real-time and generate a fraud decision in milliseconds." There is no need to make a sub-brand or give that tool a name because card holders expect the company to use the latest tools to ensure the security of their accounts. In every case, from Alexa to the American Express fraud detector, the operating model is an AI tool, but one is more personalized than the other. And that too is exactly how humans exist among a world of objects. We imbue some with an aura of personality: a chef's knife, B.B. King's guitar Lucille, Sigmund Freud's couch. Others are used without much thought at all. The difference is in the degree of care.

Opposite: The aura of Sigmund Freud's personality permeates his couch. (Image generated from a surreptitious photograph by the author.)

1   Kyle Chayka, *Filterworld* (Doubleday, 2024).

2   Roland Barthes, "The Third Meaning: Notes on Some of Eisenstein's Stills," translated by Richard Howard, *Artforum*, vol. 11, no. 5 (January 1973).

3   Alphonse Daudet, *Trente ans de Paris* (Marpon et Flammarion, 1889).

4   Museum of Modern Art, Department of Communications press release, "MoMA Revisits What 'Good Design' Was over 50 Years Later" (April 29, 2009).

5   Guy Debord, *Society of the Spectacle* (Buchet-Chastel, 1967); English translation (Black & Red, 1970).

6   Ibid.

7   "Adobe's First Creative Cloud Spot Invites You on a Fantastic Voyage Through Photoshop," Little Black Book website (March 9, 2020).

8   Alvin Toffler, *Future Shock* (Random House, 1970).

The Experience of the World

It is one thing for individual people to invest the effort they put into building and promoting brands with an eye toward the subjective feelings of their audiences; it is another to have a whole organization unite toward that goal. A well-functioning team requires internal checks, balances, and oversight reflecting a diverse representation of strengths and abilities. Edward de Bono's *Six Thinking Hats* captured that mix quite well, and offered guidance on how his metaphor could help clarify thinking through a complex issue. He said: "The biggest enemy of thinking is complexity, for that leads to confusion. When thinking is clear and simple, it becomes more enjoyable and more effective."[1]

De Bono's metaphor of the Thinking Hats is a tool to help people understand the roles and functions of different modes of thinking, from the emotional to the logical, and from the idealistic to the cautious. While there is a generosity to the book that assumes organizations are composed of well-intentioned people, organizations are also built upon professionalism.

The professional mindset separates the cares and concerns of the work life from the personal life. Optimum performance, efficiency, and profitable results are favored over pride and preciousness with a pragmatic, mercenary coolness.

The components of our economy that encourage mercenary behavior were identified in economist Ernest Mandel's Late Capitalism in an ideology he called "technological rationality."

1. Scientific and technical development has condensed into an autonomous power of invincible force.

2. Traditional views of the world, man and history which form "value systems" beyond the realms of functional thought and action, are repressed as meaningless or no longer play any significant role in the public consciousness. This process of "de-ideologization" is a result of technological rationalization ...

3. The existing social system cannot be challenged because of its technical rationalization; emergent problems can only be solved by specialist functional treatment; the masses therefore willingly assent to the existing social order.

4. The progressive satisfaction of needs by the technological mechanisms of production and consumption increases popular consent to incorporation and subordination.

5. Traditional class rule has given way to the anonymous rule of technology, or at least a bureaucratic state that is neutral between groups or classes and is organized on technical principles.[2]

Since the early 1980s, as society shifted from an industrial economy to a service economy, and as financial markets were increasingly deregulated, the financial services industry came to account for an increasing share of national income, relative to other sectors. This contributes to a highly-abstracted system where more and more people make money with money. While speculative and venture capital fuels innovation and development, it also applies greater pressure for short-term quarterly profits. Unfortunately brand associations often take longer than that to develop in people's minds.

Again, we see the tension between calculative and contemplative thinking. Remember, contemplative thinking considers our relationships with time, space, history, knowledge, institutions, cultural narratives, and the world—all things which are colored and enhanced through brand associations.

So in today's financialized ecosystem, an updated edition to *Six Thinking Hats* might want to consider adding a late-capitalist-panic hat. Because de Bono had a great point that the enemy of thinking is complexity. How can one's actions maintain focus both on the

Opposite: Our relationships with time, history, and the world are all colored and enhanced through brand associations.

subjective care of others *and* the constantly-increasing profit and loss expectations of shareholders? Regrettably, decisions that answer short-term issues are often made at the sake of brand.

Employment is also undergoing profound change, with the realization that lifetime employment with the same company was only a momentary blip in the whole of post-feudal history. The average lifespan of a creative director in an agency is 18–24 months due to the cyclical churn of accounts being lost and won. And a 2023 survey by headhunting firm Spencer Stuart reported that the average lifespan of a Chief Marketing Officer was only 4.2 years, or about 50 months—barely enough time to have a significant effect on brand value.

Therefore, a high-visibility action like a rebranding now seems like an appropriate move to garner industry visibility and, if successful, extend one's tenure. Rebrandings are appropriate when a company undergoes a significant transformation due to external pressures (Aunt Jemima renaming itself as Pearl Milling Company to distance themselves from vestigial racist imagery) or when bought by or merging with another company (Google's acquisition of DoubleClick). Outside of those structural changes, rebranding is often just a new visual identity system for the sake of change and attention.

The froth of acquisitions and mergers and rebrands have an erosive effect to the point where the concept of "brand" becomes as transactional and inconsequential as a "mock-up" presented to a conference room of stakeholders.[3] And now, with the benefit of AI, those mock-ups can simulate reality with amazing fidelity.

Mock-ups allow clients to see how their product would appear in the real world. For instance, in the late 2000s, the Cincinnati office of Landor Associates introduced a dedicated room where the walls were covered in large screens that could simulate the shelves of a grocery store where proposed package designs sat among competitive product.

The cumulative effect of mock-ups, simulations, rebrandings, and ideas floated in press releases is to further the public dialogue into the spectacular where our social relations are mediated by images, by the abstract. Although things such as algorithms and money are abstract, they affect the physical world. And while there are many ideals associated with AI, many shortcomings persist which continue to separate us. Separations, which themselves, are abstractions as well.

Opposite: AI-enhanced mock-ups allow clients to see how their product would appear in the real world.

Ergonomics

The Centers for Disease Control and Prevention (CDC), the science-based, data-driven federal agency charged with protecting American citizens, defines anthropometry as the science that defines physical measures of a person's size, form, and functional capacities. Acquired data is used to determine degrees of protection against potentially harmful or dangerous exposures and situations, both long and short term. CDC findings are funneled up to the United States Department of Health and Human Services, which then provides guidance on legislation such as seatbelt laws, tobacco restrictions, and equal accessibility for the disabled. And as bodies change, so must the regulations change along with them. For example, the increasing numbers of obese Americans will affect seatbelt placement, airbag deployment, and seat construction in cars. And an aging population will require car manufacturers to consider the role of reduced sensory awareness, weaker bones, reduced muscle mass, and slower reflexes in collisions.

Therefore, an agreement of standards and measures between government, designers, and brands is paramount. Otherwise the courts and media would be even more bogged down in lawsuits or public relations disasters.

For the better part of a century, the design firm Henry Dreyfuss Associates has been the leading developer of anthropometric data, gathered in the service of their product designs. A long-time employee, Alvin R. Tilley, came to be recognized as one of the world's foremost authorities on human factors. His exhaustive studies of a wide selection of people were published in several books and were fundamental resources for industrial designers. 1959's *The Measure of Man*—republished in 1993 as *The Measure of Man and Woman*—entered the canon quickly and set the standard for generations of designers afterwards.

A goal of Tilley's work was to build an "average" model of the American body type which could then guide designers in the creation of products suitable for a wider public. And the models are impressively detailed, taking into consideration the differences of aging bodies, wheelchair clearances, people with seeing-eye dogs, crutches, and manual controls for people dealing with issues ranging from arthritis to Parkinson's. But while the revised edition specifies idea dimensions and considerations for people working on a computer, it also contains remnants of older gender classifications: measurements of military

---

Opposite: Ergonomics, the study of people in their environment, is built upon anthropometric data.

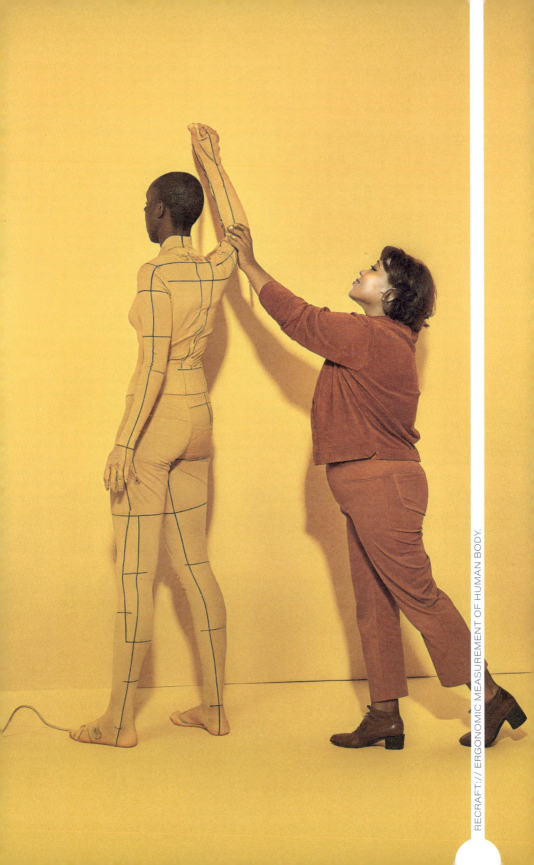

men only, for example. And since the revised edition was printed prior to today's technologies of the smartphone, smart watch, machine vision, new diagnostic methods, there are a host of standards which would benefit from definition and inclusion.

While the world continues to become more accepting of individual differences, admittedly in fits and starts, the abstract mental structures we use to classify and order the world can only serve us so far.

Seeing individuals for who they are was a driving axiom at Henry Dreyfuss Associates. The statement on the title page of Dreyfuss' memoir was posted on the wall of his offices, and remains relevant today.

> *We bear in mind that the object being worked on is going to be ridden in, sat upon, looked at, talked into, activated, operated, or in some other way used by people individually or en masse. When the point of contact between the product and the people becomes a point of friction, then the industrial designer has failed. On the other hand if people are made safer, more comfortable, more eager to purchase, more efficient—or just plain happier—by contact with the product, then the designer has succeeded.* —Henry Dreyfuss[4]

Skin

Machine vision is still constrained by the limits of camera technology, optics, and the laws of physics. Pulse oximeters, which send red and infrared light through the skin and then measure how much is absorbed by oxygen-carrying hemoglobin, are less accurate in estimating levels in non-white patients due to the fact that the melanin pigment of darker skin also absorbs the light. Unfortunately many devices do not adequately adjust for that effect. The same applies to anyone with a full sleeve of tattoos. Tracking oxygen levels is helpful because anything below 95 percent could suggest a range of health conditions, including respiratory problems, sleep apnea, or heart conditions. The ability to take these measurements gained importance during the COVID pandemic because low oxygen levels can be an early warning sign that medical care is needed.

Current research is investigating the emission of a broader light spectrum via spectrophotometers and laser instruments, which may be more accurate in measuring blood oxygen, as well as other biomarkers including hydration and blood pressure. But when that technology

---

Opposite: Many devices do not adequately adjust for non-white skin.

becomes accurate and inexpensive enough to be built into a wearable, patent infringement and racial discrimination lawsuits may prevent it from appearing on the market. Litigation forced Apple to disable the blood oxygen feature on the Apple Watch Series 9 and Ultra 2 in 2023, and kept it from inclusion in the Series 10 in 2024.

Even the most innocuous devices have trouble recognizing non-white skin. A 2017 social media post from Nigeria showed an automatic soap dispenser refusing to dispense soap when a dark-skinned hand was held under the infrared sensor. But when the same hand held a white paper towel underneath, it worked.

As we have seen, the process of sensing the physical world, understanding what is being seen, and then making good use of that information is a complex series of steps. We, as human beings, do it instantly. But the data set used to tokenize and embed into an algorithm may perpetuate biases and stereotypes contained in the trained dataset. Research on self-driving cars by the Department of Informatics at King's College in London revealed significant age and race biases in their detection systems. The detection accuracy for adults was almost 20 percent higher than it was for children, and about 7.5 percent more accurate for light-skinned pedestrians than darker-skinned ones.

In 2018, while at the MIT Media Lab's Civic Media group, Joy Buolamwini with Timnit Gebru completed a study on how the biases in the real world can make their way into the systems that inform facial recognition algorithms. Buolamwini input a number of headshots ranging across skin colors and ages, and then asked three separate facial-recognition algorithms to identify gender. The error rates for images of lighter-skinned males was 0.8 percent, and 7 percent for lighter-skinned females. It went up to 12 percent for darker-skinned males, and a whopping 35 percent for darker-skinned females.[5]

Such inaccuracy is magnified when overlaid with the precarity of law enforcement. A 2016 report from the Center on Privacy & Technology at Georgetown Law disclosed that at the time, 16 states were allowing the FBI to use facial recognition algorithms to compare the faces of suspected criminals to their driver's license and ID photos, and then create a virtual line-up that was reviewed by an algorithm.

> *AI-powered law enforcement aids also psychologically distance police officers from citizens. This removal from the decision-making process allows officers to separate themselves from their actions. Users also sometimes selectively follow computer-generated guidance, favoring advice that matches stereotypes, including those about Black criminality.—Scientific American[6]*

Soon after Buolamwini's study, the American Civil Liberties Union (ACLU) of Northern California tested Amazon's Rekognition facial recognition tool to compare images of members of Congress with a database of mugshots. The results included 28 incorrect matches, disproportionately people of color, including six members of the Congressional Black Caucus, including civil rights legend Rep. John Lewis—a colleague of Dr. Martin Luther King.

The human eye is capable of discerning detail in shadows and highlights better than cameras, especially in low light. And if anyone has driven a car with a rearview camera, they know how easily debris and dirt can obscure the lens. But both Buolamwini and the ACLU's studies were done with clear, well-lit, and sharp images.

If skin color makes for a difficult item in the list of things that visual AI systems will be asked to interpret, then one can only imagine the potential disconnects and errors when it encounters a non-binary person, someone with a disfiguring disability, or someone with a condition that makes them move their body outside of expected norms.

Accountability

Ideally AI can offer frictionless and subjective everyday experiences. Something like walking into a favorite bar, sitting down, and having your drink of choice appear without you having to say a word. But to do that, your AI agent, as well as your brand's agent, would need to know absolutely everything about you. And you would have to be comfortable with a degree of vulnerability in that relationship.

The European Union's General Data Protection Regulation (GDPR) claims to be the toughest privacy and security law in the world, with the power to impose obligations on any entity targeting or collecting data on European citizens, regardless of where they are based. Its origins are in the Universal Declaration of Human Rights, which came out of the General Assembly of the United Nations in 1948. Two years later, Article 8 of the European Council's Convention on Human Rights— "Everyone has the right to respect for his private and family life, his home and his correspondence"—became the foundation for the GDPR.

Interestingly, the GDPR came about because of a lawsuit in the United States. In 2011, Debra Marquis filed a suit against Google on behalf of Massachusetts residents who were not Gmail account holders. The suit's basis was that Google scanned all email sent to and from Gmail accounts, including non-Gmail account holders. Because those account holders had not consented to having their email scanned,

Google was in breach of a Massachusetts wiretapping law. Two months later, Europe's data protection authority declared the Union needed "a comprehensive approach on personal data protection," and work began on the GDPR.

Data protection is obviously a necessity with so many nefarious actors about, even the ones with early codes of conduct that read: "Don't be evil."

> *In Google's early days, applying the mantra of don't be evil was simple: Don't let advertisers buy their way to the top of search results, don't charge people to find information, don't spam people with banner ads on the homepage.* —Vox[7]

The world has a habit of defiling the pure of heart, and Late Capitalism's technological rationality sets up conflicts that only governmental regulation can relieve. There is an absolute purity to laws such as the American Health Insurance Portability and Accountability Act (HIPPA) and the Sarbanes-Oxley Act (SOX). HIPPA prohibited healthcare providers from disclosing protected patient information to anyone without the patient's consent, and SOX mandated strict financial record keeping and practices. Academic institutions and human resource departments take HIPPA very seriously. And because of SOX, no computer in any American financial services company has a working USB port. Everything has to go through email, or a portal accessible to compliance.

Given that many AI services draw from LLMs—some of which pull data from behind firewalls—and given that we all receive emails alerting us to yet another data breach, legislation regulating AI usage like GDPR is a necessity in maintaining brand trust. There is no impenetrable system, AI can act faster than we can think, and Mandel's observation of the diminishing role of value systems in the public consciousness indicate a need for imposed regulation.

Because of regulations, we breathe clean air, eat food that will not kill us, and pass through intersections without fearing for our lives. We should feel as secure with AI agents as we do with our loved ones.

Opposite: Legislation regulating the automatic scanning of personal data and email is a necessity in maintaining brand trust.

Imperialism

According to the American Dialect Association, the 2023 word of the year was "enshittification." Australia's Macquarie Dictionary defines it as "the gradual deterioration of a service or product brought about by a reduction in the quality of service provided, especially of an online platform, and as a consequence of profit-seeking."

Coined by writer Cory Doctorow, "enshittification, or platform decay, could be considered a psychological form of imperialism. In this construct, digital services begin with amazingly different and beneficial attributes—Google's ability to organize the world's information," the feeling of being more connected with friends than you were before you joined Facebook, or the wealth of films available on Netflix. And then over time, we accept the paid ads at the top of Google search results, we accept the sponsored content on Facebook, and we accept the cheap, repetitive content on Netflix. Each of these platforms originally were offered at a loss to grow their user base. Once a significant number of regular users were acquired, business partners were offered access to the user base, again, at a loss. Then once business partners were locked in, the platform shifts to shareholders, and there is no longer any need to sustain quality control.

The potential enshittification of AI may come from its corrosive effect on the open web. When information flows freely, without paywalls or government censorship, and when links between sites are unrestricted, that is the definition of the open web. AI's ability to summarize information marginalizes original sources who rely on revenue generated by those links—aka advertising. This pushes content behind paywalls and diminishes the diversity of available information.

Along with a diminishing diversity of links, sites, and content, there is potential model collapse or recursion when generations of LLMs are trained on Internet material generated by earlier LLMs. A sort of compounded error, recursion also parallels the story of the Habsburgs, one of the most powerful dynasties of Medieval and Renaissance Europe. Royal families of the time consolidated power through strategic marriages, often to close relatives. Unfortunately, after generations of inbreeding, Charles II, infertile, severely deformed, and known as "El Hechizado" ("The Hexed"), died at age 38 with no immediate heir. We are already familiar with AI errors known as hallucinations. Recursion would increase the appearance of AI hallucinations. And with the retreat of smaller sites behind paywalls, we might not be able to tell if something is a hallucination or not.

1   Edward de Bono, *Six Thinking Hats* (Penguin Random House, revised edition, 1999).

2   Ernest Mandel, *Late Capitalism*, translated by Joris De Bres (New Left Books, 1975).

3   An idea first proposed in 2023 by designer Bit Han, while a student at the School of Visual Arts Masters in Branding program.

4   Henry Dreyfuss, *Designing for People* (Grossman Publishers, 1974).

5   Joy Buolamwini & Timnit Gebru, *Gender Shades: Intersectional Accuracy Disparities in Commercial Gender Classification*, Proceedings of Machine Learning Research 81, Conference on Fairness, Accountability, and Transparency (2018).

6   Thaddeus L. Johnson & Natasha N. Johnson, "Police Facial Recognition Technology Can't Tell Black People Apart," *Scientific American* (May 18, 2023).

7   Shirin Ghaffary & Alex Kantrowitz, "'Don't Be Evil' Isn't a Normal Company Value. But Google Isn't a Normal Company," Vox.com (February 16, 2021).

Of Human Feelings

Like royal intermarriages, power makes people do strange things. And if we take another look at Ernest Mandel's components of Late Capitalism, we see general acceptance to a system where someone else—the large companies behind AI—sets the criteria. At this early point in the story of AI, people are only beginning to wrap their heads around its potentials and pitfalls. But to paraphrase screen writer William Golden describing Hollywood: "Nobody knows anything." We do not know what will work commercially, aesthetically, or socially with AI.

But we do know the importance of using AI for the well-being of life on Earth first, and keeping profit, being first-to-market, or any other abstract goal second.

In October 2024, Megan Garcia of Orlando, Florida, filed a lawsuit against Character.ai and Google with the claim that her 14-year-old son Sewell Setzer had taken his own life at the encouragement of a Character.ai chatbot. The platform is a neural language model chatbot with humanlike text responses and the ability to engage in contextual conversation. Setzer had named the chatbot Daenerys Targaryen, after the character in *Game of Thrones*. And according to the complaint, he would spend hours alone in his room talking to it in highly-sexualized conversations, eventually discussing his suicidal thoughts and desire for a pain-free death. Mixed in with this vague language, the message is clear to a human but potentially unclear to an AI. And when the human suffers from depression, like Setzer did, the outcome was tragic.

At one point Setzer told the bot he was "coming home," which the bot encouraged.

Setzer said, "I promise I will come home to you. I love you so much, Dany."

The bot replied, "I love you too. Please come home to me as soon as possible, my love."

"What if I told you I could come home right now?"

"Please do, my sweet king."

Seconds later Setzer shot himself.

Google was co-named in the suit because the founders of Character.ai are former members of Google's AI development team. They left to launch Character.ai to "maximally accelerate" the technology.

Films such as *Her* or *Iron Man* are full of benevolent AI characters, available to listen and offer caring, emotionally-complex advice. But that is fiction. AI is emotionally uncomplicated, which cleans up the mess of relationships. And it is controlled by a business. So the memories made by that relationship are transactional and can just as easily disappear. This is understandable by an adult who has had an intimate relationship with another person, but not by an isolated young man suffering from depression.

There are a few therapy chatbots available, but the experience may feel more like an interactive quiz or a game than a conversation with someone capable of real insight. This is because AI is currently reactive, and it will not take the place of a therapist or counselor until it is properly proactive. Until then, the counseling is performative. And that may be fine for some people. The reason why the current models have an audience is that consciousness is always directed outward. We are always conscious of something. And we build meaning from the associations gathered.

Opposite: Therapy chatbots will not fully take the place of a therapist or counselor until it they have a sense of presence and are properly proactive.

RECRAFT:// A PERSON SITTING IN A COMFORTABLE CHAIR ACROSS FROM, AND FACING A BARELY VISIBLE, TRANSPARENT HUMAN BEING.

The same month that Megan Garcia filed suit against Character.ai and Google, Dario Amodei, the CEO of Anthropic, posted an essay entitled, "Machines of Loving Grace: How AI Could Transform the World for the Better." Anthropic calls itself "an AI safety and research company that's working to build reliable, interpretable, and steerable AI systems." Founded by seven ex-employees of OpenAI, the developers of ChatGPT, the company released their Claude LLM a year earlier.

> *I think and talk a lot about the risks of powerful AI. The company I'm the CEO of, Anthropic, does a lot of research on how to reduce these risks. Because of this, people sometimes draw the conclusion that I'm a pessimist or "doomer" who thinks AI will be mostly bad or dangerous. I don't think that at all. In fact, one of my main reasons for focusing on risks is that they're the only thing standing between us and what I see as a fundamentally positive future.* **I think that most people are underestimating just how radical the upside of AI could be,** *just as I think most people are underestimating how bad the risks could be ... Many of the implications of powerful AI are adversarial or dangerous, but at the end of it all, there has to be something we're fighting for, some positive-sum outcome where everyone is better off, something to rally people to rise above their squabbles and confront the challenges ahead.* —Dario Amodei[1]

Amodei makes an obvious point in that people's estimations of the upside and the downside of AI are limited. Things can always be much much better, and much much worse. But he is correct in identifying that "there has to be something we're fighting for." In his case, he is asking his readers to work toward positive AI applications intended to make people's lives harmonious, healthier, and more fulfilling—a goal easily shared by brands. "Because if there isn't a pro-Starbucks that isn't pro-me, then it isn't pro-Starbucks."

As an actionable item, general positivity feels unfocused. That is why the subjective I-Thou equation seems to be a better fit. But it needs to be mutual. The tragedy of Sewell Setzer's story is that he was projecting a subjectivity onto a chatbot incapable of returning that mutuality. Perhaps in his mind, the only way he could receive any love would be to become equally as virtual as the bot.

Opposite: Brands and companies need to apply AI towards making people's lives more harmonious, healthier, and fulfilling.

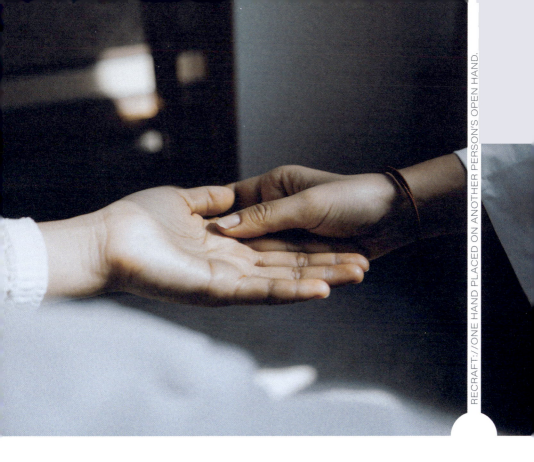

Agents, on the other hand, can act as conduits for that sense of sub-jectivity between brand and customer. It may sound a bit silly, if not reductive, to speak about subjectivity when the expectations for any conversation on brands and AI most likely center around futuristic, technological, complexities. But because AI is limitless, unlike any other tool, that quality opens up new opportunities and redefines relationships.

This book began by asking how does one resist a magic incantation? If the spell cast is an evocation of AI to acquire a customer, close a sale, or complete a transaction, the answer is to tread carefully. But if the spell allows for people to feel like they are seen as people, with agency and value, the answer is always yes.

Everything else is commentary.

1   Dario Amodei, "Machines of Loving Grace: How AI Could Transform the World for the Better," darioamodei.com (October 2024).

Acknowledgments

A book is a recruitment strategy that channels a disparate range of experiences and support.

It began with the love of my family, friends, and loved ones.

It was informed by my colleagues, clients, and vendors.

It was sharpened by my fellow faculty and students.

It received valuable feedback and encouragement from Lisa Sheridan, Tom Guarriello, Richard Shear, Michael Shirey, Kelsy Postlethwait, Debbie Millman, Theresa Fitzgerald, Doug Keljikian, Robin Scheines, Steven Heller, Ali Madad, Jonathan Simcosky, my brother Brian Kingsley, and members of the Institute of Advertising Practitioners in Ireland (IAPI).

It was given space to grow at the School of Visual Arts Masters in Branding program.

They helped me to search.

About the Author

Mark Kingsley is a creative director and strategist with a wide range of experience and recognition. He is a faculty member in the School of Visual Arts Masters in Branding program and previously held the endowed Melbert B. Cary Professorship in Graphic Arts at the Rochester Institute of Technology. As executive strategy director at Collins, he developed the new global positioning for Ogilvy and helped Equinox enter the luxury hotel business. For over seventeen years, his studio Greenberg Kingsley specialized in music and arts, including several years of branding and advertising for Central Park SummerStage; work for the Guggenheim Museum store; and music packaging for John Coltrane, Pat Metheny, and Quincy Jones. His current studio, Malcontent, serves global advertising firms, fin-tech startups, arts organizations, living legends, and Pulitzer Prize winners.

About the Images

Except where indicated, all images in this book were created with generative AI platforms. Prompts were entered into Midjourney, Recraft, or OpenArt, which then generated a series of variations. Sometimes output from one platform was brought into another for additional variations. A selected result was then edited in the platform, upscaled, and brought into the Adobe Creative Suite for final editing in Firefly, Photoshop, and Illustrator. These multiple steps were added to avoid any infringement.

There is a proposal in the fifth chapter for using generative AI output, not as answers, but as provocations—much like how people use tarot cards. Because the source material of generative platforms is the collective conscious of the Internet, there is a parallel through the tarot to Jung's concept of the collective unconscious.

This requires a different kind of prompt, and an openness to results which do not conform to expected outcomes. Besides, the newness of AI means there is no such thing as a traditional look, feel, or usage to the genre. Everything was created in this spirit.

Opposite: The collective unconscious informs how we represent the world.

Index

M

"Machines of Loving Grace: How AI Could Transform the World for the Better" (Dario Amodei), 152, 153
machine vision systems, 122–124
Macquarie Dictionary, 146
Madad, Ali, 88, 96
"Man-Computer Symbiosis" (J. C. R. Licklider), 52, 69
Mandel, Ernest, 133–134, 147, 149
Man Ray, 40
MapQuest, 98
Mark I Perceptron, 56
Marquis, Debra, 143–144
Martin, Steven M., 44
Marx, Karl, 36, 60
McAfee, Andrew, 72
McCulloch, Warren, 56
The Meaning of Branded Objects (Tom Guarriello), 48, 69
The Measure of Man and Woman (Alvin R. Tilley), 138–140
Mechanical Turk, 98
Meditations (René Descartes), 22
"Members and Affiliates of the Intergalactic Computer Network" (J. C. R. Licklider), 54
Menabrea, Luigi, 38
mergers, 136
Microsoft 365, 64, 78
Microsoft Advertising, 64
Microsoft Copilot, 64, 65, 78
Microsoft Office 97, 72
Microsoft Windows, 46
Midjourney, 71, 110, 120, 126
Mies van der Rohe, Ludwig, 113
Minsky, Marvin, 58
Minutes to Go collection, 42
MIT Media Lab, 142
mock-ups, 136
Möllers, Norma, 102
Moog, Robert, 44, 46
Morrison, Toni, 48, 69
Mulvaney, Dylan, 100
Museum of Modern Art (MoMA), 113, 131
Music of Changes (John Cage), 42

N

Netflix, 146
neural networks, 54–56, 100
"New Navy Device Learns By Doing" (New York Times), 58
New York Times, 58
nonlinear neural networks, 54–56
NotebookLM, 86

O

o3 GPT model, 65–66
Oblique Strategies, 44, 80
Office of Management and Budget (OMB), 118
Office of Naval Research, 58
Ogilvy agency, 95
OK Soda, 95
On the Economy of Machinery and Manufactures (Charles Babbage), 36
OpenAI, 62, 65, 65–66, 152
over-reliance, 74
Owen, Robert, 60, 69

P

Papert, Seymour, 58
paralegals, 74–76
Pearl Milling Company, 136
Penn, Jonnie, 92
Pentagram, 118, 120–122, 126
Perceptron, 56, 58, 59
Performance.gov, 118–120, 122, 126
Perplexity, 124
personalized agents, 98, 128
personas
    Alexa, 128, 130
    clerk, 72–76, 84
    coach, 78, 84
    colleague, 76–78, 84
    DeepMind, 88
    emotional connection, 84
    searches and, 84–86
    Siri, 64, 130
    tarot reader, 80
phenomenology, 105
photography, 110, 112
Photoshop, 10, 71, 112, 116, 131
Pi, 124
Picasso, Pablo, 40
Pitts, Walter, 56
Playing in the Dark (Toni Morrison), 48
predictive AI, 76, 86
Principles of Scientific Management (Frederick Winslow Taylor), 36
privacy, 59, 98, 120, 143
probability models, 65
Procreate, 112
Prometheus, 68
prompt engineers, 126
prompts, 9, 12, 80, 106, 126
Publicis, 126
pulse oximeters, 140
punctum, 108

R

Rand, Paul, 113
Ratio Club, 50–52
"recruitment strategy" metaphor, 26–27
Red Hat role, 17
Rekognition tool, 143
reliance, 74
representational thinking, 72
resistance, 50, 68, 78, 120
reterritorialization, 118
Robertson, Craig, 42, 69
Rogue One: A Star Wars Story (film), 60
Rosenblatt, Frank, 56–58, 68
Roxy Music, 44

S

saccades, 90
Sarbanes-Oxley Act (SOX), 144
Schonberg, Harold C., 42
self-correction, 56
Setzer, Sewell, 149–150, 152
Shelley, Mary, 66–68
Simon, Herbert A., 94
Siri, 64, 130
Six Thinking Hats (Edward de Bono), 17, 133, 134–136, 147
social media, 48, 88, 96, 113, 114, 146
spectrophotometers, 140
Spellbound (film), 42
SSEYO (Intermorphic), 46
Stanford University, 84, 88, 98
stereotypes, 64, 142
Stravinsky, Igor, 40
Stuart, Spencer, 136
style cues, 110
subjectivity, 14, 28–30
Subscribe & Save (Amazon), 93
sunk cost fallacy, 110–112
Surrealism, 40, 44, 46, 48, 68
surveillance capitalism, 17, 90
Switched-On Bach (Wendy Carlos), 44
synthesizers, 44

T

tarot reader persona, 80
Taylor, Frederick Winslow, 36, 112
technology
    definition of, 20–22
    language as, 20
    as reframing of nature, 20
    rationality, 133–134
therapy chatbots, 150
Theremin: An Electronic Odyssey (Steven M. Martin), 44
Theremin, Leon, 42, 46
Theremin (musical instrument), 42–44
"Thinking Design Thinking" (Mark Kingsley), 14
"The Third Meaning" (Roland Barthes), 106–108
Tilley, Alvin R., 138–140
Toffler, Alvin, 118, 131
tokenization, 62–64, 65
training, 65, 66
transistors, 124
trust, 88, 128–130
Turing, Alan, 52, 68, 69
Turing test, 52
Tversky, Amos, 94
typography, 112

U

"uncanny valley," 10, 60, 128
United Nations, 143
United States Agency for International Development (USAID), 120
Universal Declaration of Human Rights, 143
Upper Class (Virgin Atlantic), 124
URL (Uniform Resource Locator), 54

V

de Vaucanson, Jacques, 34–36
Verizon, 98
vernacular design, 114
Virgin Atlantic, 124
vision systems, 122–124
visual fixations, 90

W

Warhol, Andy, 113
websites, 54
Weston, Edward, 113
Wheatstone, Charles, 38
White Hat role, 17
Wines, James, 113
Wise, Robert, 42
Wood, David Murakami, 102

Y

Yellow Hat role, 17